A GREEK PROMISE

A journey of faith

BARBARA GILIS

Scripture is taken from the Holy Bible, New International Version

This book is non-fiction. In some cases names of people and places have been altered to protect their privacy.

ISBN: 978-960-93-9596-0

DEDICATION

To the people of Paros who have welcomed me and
shared their island and their lives with me; I thank you.

.

CONTENTS

This book, the Greek promise, was given to Jager e Tonia, from yiayia on the May 24-20

Loula's testimony, is under All Nations, on page 157 and it starts, on the page 161, where it says:
God had promised to me ...
...... e it is finish on page 167, e the man, who she is talking at the end, is my brother Nick, and the Lady, was my sister Maria, three of us, we were travelling to Paros e there in the boat, we met Barbara.
God is doing miracles today. Believe in him
All His Blessings
with His Love, yiayia Loula

ACKNOWLEDGMENTS

I wish to thank my parents, Roy and Olive Butler, who made the sacrifice to lose their daughter to faraway Greece.

I am deeply indebted to Lizzie North who has edited this manuscript and to my dear husband Peter for his patient support and his part in this story.

BARBARA GILIS

PREFACE

A Greek Promise is an inspiring account of how God still calls ordinary people to do extraordinary things. The many miraculous events are intertwined with endearing descriptions of the delights of Greek life that have produced popular Greek based books by other authors. This unusual combination sets the scene for this true story, providing a delightful adventure for believers and sceptics alike. Courage, faith, compassion and a child-like dependence on God's provision form the backdrop to this enchanting Greek island, modern day epistle. The story relates the most amazing events which defy any explanation other than that they were determined and controlled by the actions of an Almighty God.

My previous book, *To Greece and the Distant Islands*, relates the fascinating events which first led me, an English business woman in her late thirties, to leave home and move to live a simple life on a Greek island. Many of the readers of that book asked, "But then what happened?" It is in answer to this question that this second book has been written including events up to the present day.

1 A GREEK HOME

Fewer than ten years had passed since I had closed the door on my English life and arrived on the island of Paros. There was absolutely no area of my life unchanged

Having lived the single life on the Piso Livadi campsite for two summers, married back in England and then lived a further two years in a rented house in the village of Marpissa, it was wonderful to finally have a real home. There was such a sense of achievement for both of us, my husband, Peter, having built it brick by brick.

We had the most beautiful views from the spacious terraces built around the east and south sides of the house. These afforded clear views down to the beach and across the sparkling blue Aegean to the adjacent island of Naxos.

Each morning the sun rose over the mountains of Naxos facing our Logaras bay. It then crept to the south of the house until it finally plunged dramatically behind the mountains of Paros to the west.

Not to be outdone, every twenty-eight days the full moon would delight us by rising in an orange blaze of regal splendour silhouetting the Naxos mountain tops. In later years, the local Fisilani restaurant on the beach would give this event the glory it deserved by playing Zorba's Dance just as the moon first peeped over the mountain. Tiny tea lights were then floated on the tranquil sea creating an intoxicating atmosphere for diners and lovers together.

With almost no buildings or street lights the stars above twinkled brightly, completing this masterpiece, this canopy of creation. Thankfully, our house has a staircase to a flat roof which, at special times of the year, makes a great place to lie and watch the shooting stars fall to the earth.

In those early days, the summer evenings were long and balmy. Serenaded by the cicadas, we would sit at our simple camping table on the unpaved terrace soaking in the peace and tranquillity. To us it felt like a banqueting table in a palace. At last I had my "someone special" to share life with.

It didn't matter at all that life was rather simple. I cooked on a two-ring gas hob, which, after using a spirit burner on the campsite for two years, was luxury indeed. I had a full kitchen rather than keeping my food supplies in the Land Rover, and an electric fridge rather than one powered from the car battery.

Each morning we stepped out of our front door onto bare dust and stones. It would take years of toil to transform the arid terrain and coax the dry dust into a garden with fruit and flowers. In the early days, our budget didn't stretch to buying flowers so we took lots of geranium cuttings from friends and just stuck them in the ground. Amazingly, they always took and then grew fifty to seventy centimetres high. Unlike in England, here they can stay out all winter, there is absolutely no need to bring them inside to a greenhouse. We live in a greenhouse!

Immediately outside the front door, our Parian architect had rather creatively designed a spacious courtyard, or *avli* as it is called in Greek, so that was Peter's next project. The two metre high wall would protect us from both north and south winds. The traditional entrance with a relieving triangle above is a classic Greek feature making the house look authentically Greek. Peter then built a corner bench inside the *avli* just perfect for taking his afternoon siesta in the shade of the wall. Our dog, Abee, would settle down with him and they would snooze happily together until it was time for a swim. Over the years the courtyard became home to a magnificent red bougainvillea, a white jasmine and a purple wisteria. With the final addition of a *nichta louloudi*, a Greek night flower, it all added to the heady perfume as we relaxed in the cool of the evening.

Abee found the freedom of life outside the village a sheer delight. Apart from his bi-annual "go find a girl event", he was well trained and never chased sheep or goats. His reward for this was to be free to run on the beach and outside the house, though we always kept him in sight. He would never be one of those Greek dogs who spend their whole life on a chain at the bottom of the garden.

Each morning when Peter had work we would be up at six thirty. I'd prepare his breakfast, pack his sandwiches for lunch and polish his boots. It seemed the least I could do when he would work outside in the hot sun all day. As I filled his thermos with cool water each morning, a silent enemy was accumulating stones in his kidneys. The calcium in the water would gradually form stones that would bring him to his knees in agony.

Our water supply from the tap in our house was often an orange trickle full of sand dirt. Way back in the Marpissa days, we had learnt to travel to the spring in the mountains to collect our water. We call it "Spring Valley" and what a delightful place it is with its small Orthodox church, surrounded by Cypress trees, nestling on the side of the hill. There were very few trees on the island at that time, so it was a shady haven of peace. We would drive up with ten litre water containers and fill them from the tap installed in a simple stone hut. For us it was quite a climb; the locals could take their donkey, but, even for a Land

Rover, driving was out of the question. In later years, a pipe ran the water to a more accessible spot, though still way outside the village, and then we were able to drive up and take our empty one-and-a-half-litre water bottles in red Coca Cola crates. The place swarmed with wasps eager to drink in the cool of the evening so, for someone like me with a terrible fear of wasps, it was a great lesson in overcoming fear when needs must! Both sources were supplied from the island's marble water table. The marble, composed of calcium carbonate, was to become the cause of serious problems for Peter. In a typical day's work of seven to eight hours, Peter would drink several litres to slake his thirst in the searing heat.

The wages he was paid were pitiful but we had to eat and that was the work that was available. He would work seven hours for just seven thousand drachmas – about twenty-one euros – which is just three euros an hour. Other retired friends with a pension or a good income, and who didn't need to work, would often sit enjoying a coffee in the harbour during the day. I couldn't even think about such a luxury when I knew how long Peter would have to work to pay for my coffee. It was a far cry from the days when I earned more per hour than he was paid for a day, but neither of us had come to Paros for the money. We were happy and life seemed very good to us at the time.

By four o'clock he would come home and our work for the day was finished. We would stroll down to the beach for a swim, the beach being just at the end of the road. Peter was rapidly becoming an expert at harpooning octopus and would slowly float around the nooks and crannies in the rocks to spot their hidey holes. He discovered that small piles of rocks in front of a larger rock usually indicated the house of an octopus which had piled up the stones to disguise the entrance. The small fish swimming around tended to give the game away. Often, poking it with the harpoon, the octopus would just creep further in until our dinner vanished silently into the hole.

In later years, he was given a tip on how to entice the octopus out of its hiding place by breaking sea urchins just close to the entrance. Now, the temptation to come out and eat them and the fish that they attracted was just too great to resist. The octopus would creep out and… "whoosh"… Peter would thrust forward with the harpoon and grab it. Then it was time for stage two, smashing it on the rocks to tenderise it, having first killed it of course. It is not uncommon in Greece to see local fishermen rolling a bunch of ten or more octopus on the rocks until white foam appears. That's stage three. It's all part of the tenderising process, although one does wonder how they ever discovered that.

After a swim and a nap we would be free to join our local friends and visiting tourists at the beachside café. Unlike the Marpissa days, we used the Land Rover less and less; it was marvellous to be able to walk everywhere. This of course required plenty of time, not for the walking but rather to stop and talk to each person we passed. Everyone was greeted by their first names: "Yiasou Maria, yiasou Stefanos"; yiasou meaning "your health", which is the standard form of greeting. It was quite unthinkable to hurry anywhere without enquiring how they were and if were they well. On their visits, my mum and dad found it astonishing that we knew each person by name.

Winter was a whole different scenario. The tourists were gone, the rooms and restaurants were closed, and the local people rested after having worked a double shift the whole summer. Stoves were lit; those lucky enough to be able to afford central heating and the oil to run it flicked their boiler switch on and most people just snuggled down at home for the evening. The older Greeks seemed to think heating was an unnecessary luxury so visits to their houses required several layers of clothing. It wasn't so much that the temperature fell much below ten degrees, but the humidity was often seventy or eighty percent. Many older people experienced joint pain in their shoulders or hips. The humidity also caused mildew to climb up the concrete pillars in the corners of rooms as the concrete sucked up the water from the earth. There was no such thing as a damp-course, unless you built without a concrete frame and risked the whole building crashing on your head during an earthquake. The only thing to do was to bleach the walls every three weeks wherever the mildew grew. Fortunately, I had Peter to do that. I had visited houses where people were unable to do it themselves and the whole ceiling had turned black!

It was on these winter evenings that our short Greek farmer friend, Manolis, would limp down the road, tapping his way with his olive wood stick. A bag of whatever he wanted to share with us would dangle at his side. Our woodstove kept our lounge well above twenty degrees and we also had a television. In those early days Manolis had no electricity in his simple stable like room at the end of our street. His favourite TV soap, *Lampsi,* was something we never watched, but, for the sake of friendship, we couldn't refuse his request to turn it on. He would usually bring us a large water bottle filled with his goat's milk for us to make a local soft Mezithra cheese. Alternatively, he might bring some of his own wine from his huge barrel in the stable.

One night, he carefully produced several eggs from his pocket and laid them on the kitchen unit. He then settled down by the stove to watch *Lampsi.* About half an hour later I noticed something yellow oozing from his jacket pocket. After I had brought this to his attention, he explained that he hadn't liked to give us the egg he broke on the way down the street. Carrying fresh eggs from the bakery in a paper bag was yet another new skill essential to Greek life which I had learnt. I experienced such a sense of achievement when arriving home with all ten intact, a triumph forfeited when buying them in plastic boxes from the supermarket.

Our Greek goatherd, Manolis, really was so sweet and

he seemed to have taken us under his wing; after all, that's what neighbours are for. He taught us how to collect *horta*, wild greens like dandelions, and then boil them before drizzling or drenching them in olive oil and lemon. We had our own young olive trees at this stage but it would take a few years before we had our own annual crop of oil. In the meantime, we could only buy small bottles from the supermarket. It seemed that olive oil was one of the only things that Greeks don't share, even if they have two hundred litres. On the other hand, lemons, courgettes, tomatoes, cheese, milk and wine were showered upon us. In later years, we typically had thirty litres of oil annually, but on one occasion we even had ninety litres, the reward for picking the olives from a friend's one hundred olive trees. It took the two of us five days.

Manolis also showed us where to find *karfa*, a wild asparagus appearing in May. After the early rains we also collected snails and fed them flour to clean them before cooking. The vital piece of local knowledge was what kind of container to keep them in without suffocating them, yet prevent them from escaping and crawling into every nook and cranny in the kitchen! On my first attempt it took hours to find them all. Without doubt, our favourite of all the wild foods he showed us were the mushrooms. They popped up freely in the surrounding fields a few weeks after the first rains. We collected them by the bagful and then checked them with our other farmer friend, Adonis, who taught us how to identify the edible varieties from the poisonous. Only in Greece do you have the challenge of what to do with two carrier bags full of mushrooms or six carrier bags full of lemons. It certainly is the land of plenty on the islands.

2 OUR ALBANIAN FAMILY

It was during our second summer living on Logaras when we had rather unexpected visitors. Our Albanian family arrived on the doorstep having travelled from Athens and then over from the main town on the morning bus. Yannis and Vera had occasionally joined us on Sunday mornings two years earlier. Yannis, the husband, was tall, slim and dark; Vera was shorter, a homely mother of three. This time, their eight year old daughter, Irini, and their new son, Elkioni, were with them. Their eldest son, Eros, would join them later. They had come to Paros to try to find work, having lived in Athens for a while since their previous visit. They were hopeful that we might be able to find them work and a place to live. As it was a Saturday morning when they arrived, finding work was unlikely to happen the same day, so we offered to put them up for a few days. Although we didn't have a spare bedroom, we did have a dining room separate to our lounge, so for sure we could put some mattresses on the floor for them. They at least had a room to themselves

My immediate concern was that it was Sunday the next day. As foreigners, attending the Greek Orthodox Church wasn't really an option: we couldn't understand the old *Katherevousa* Greek language, didn't know the Byzantian chants and we weren't allowed to share the communion of bread and wine. So it had become our custom to meet in our home with any other foreigners who wanted to worship and read the Bible in English. How on earth was I going to manage to teach on the Bible in Greek, our only common language, at such short notice? What worship songs could we use when we sang usually in English? In the end, Gill, who is married to a Greek, was more than able to translate and, in order to get to know each other better, we all shared our stories of how and when we had become Christians. We knew better than to be deceived into thinking it was just something that happened at infant baptism.

"Love one another" seemed to be the message for the day. We also took the opportunity to thank God for the various people healed earlier in the week at the meetings with Liberis, a visiting Greek South African church pastor from Athens.

Liberis was the pastor who had come to pray with me in the Athens hospital where I had been operated on for breast cancer. He had just been to visit Paros with his family for two days. On one of the evenings a group of ten of us had gathered to hear God's Word on healing and salvation and to pray together. As he ministered to us, I fell to the ground under the power of the Holy Spirit and was completely at peace as the Holy Spirit worked in my body, my mind and my emotions. God was continuing the healing in my body that had begun when Peter and I first prayed together after discovering an apparent lump in my remaining breast. A German lady, who had a thyroid problem, felt the power of God on her body as we prayed together. Doreen, a retired English lady, gently fell to the ground as the Holy Spirit moved amongst us, just as I had done the day before. Several people were healed and some rededicated their lives to Christ. Others received Christ as their Saviour for the first time. Fortunately, my breast was diagnosed as hormonal lumps not a tumour. Having just had surgery for breast cancer and suffered the removal of my left breast, I certainly didn't want to repeat the whole experience again.

So now Vera shared with us how she had been going to a church in Athens for two years from 1990 and had received Christ as her Saviour in 1992. It was 1994 when she had first come to Paros and she and Yannis had visited us without the children.

That same evening, three Kenyan girls – Eva, Polly and Lilly – came to visit. Eva and Lilly had been with us on Sundays the year before but Polly was new to the island. Lilly had found a job at Pounda Beach paying 4,000 drachmas for an eight hour day. That is about twelve euros, or just one and a half euros an hour. It was, in fact, the same wages they had paid me six years earlier in 1990 when I first came to Paros, and there was still no increase being offered!

All three of them said they had not been born again but they did believe Jesus was the Son of God and that God had raised Him from the dead. With that foundational belief, it was a simple matter to preach the gospel to them and lead them in a prayer to receive Christ as their Lord and Saviour, just as I had done all those years before in England. Regrettably, we didn't baptise them that evening or pray for them to be baptised in the Holy Spirit and receive the gift of tongues, as the Apostle Paul did in the book of Acts chapter 16. I still had a lot to learn.

Life as a large family in our three-roomed house was a challenge for all of us, especially for Yannis who was working extremely long hours. He had found a job with the husband of an English friend of mine and was painting houses. In the Cyclades islands all the exterior walls are painted white and, with the blistering summer sun, the doors and window frames need painting frequently. The particular job he was doing was on the smaller, adjacent island of Antiparos. This meant taking the car ferry across each day. With an hour to get there and an hour to return late in the evening after the light had faded, it was often 11p.m. by the time he arrived home. The dear man barely had time to eat and sleep before starting all over again the next day.

In the meantime, Vera and I were going around the local area looking at houses for rent. Of course they all belonged to people we knew, our neighbours on Logaras and nearby. Eventually, Vera chose the village house of our neighbours, Yannis and Elefanta, an elderly Greek couple who had rooms in the river valley below our house. They also owned an older, traditional style house in the village of Marpissa, which had a garden for the children to play in. It was about one kilometre from our house on Logaras. At least it would give them a life of their own and the rent, at a quarter of Yannis' total wage, would leave them enough for food, electricity and water. It was a start.

Looking back, I would have to say I was very grateful for the opportunity to have Yannis and Vera and the children living with us for that month. It was the beginning of a friendship that would last for years. We baptised Vera and I taught Irini English for many years. She passed her Cambridge English Certificate exam and, eventually, even the Proficiency level exam, although by then she was taking lessons at the local *Frontistirio*, which is the Greek name for private tuition schools. Irini became the daughter I never had and, being very bright, was a pleasure to teach. As they moved house around the village, ever improving their situation, Peter and I were always welcome visitors. We were invited to many a lovely meal with the family and Vera made the best *Spanakopita* (spinach pie) of anyone I knew.

Many years later, Vera and Irini moved up to Athens so that Irini could take up an offer of special athletics coaching, as she was a top sprinter in her age group. She had excelled in several events in the local Cyclades

11

competitions where she had been talent spotted. Her two brothers were equally promising as boy protégé football players; later, they too moved to Athens to go to schools where they could attend special football coaching. Their father Yannis had been a professional football player in Albania and his high standard in coaching Irini and the boys had borne fruit.

Later, Elkioni (re-baptised Giorgos) and Eros (re-baptised Vasili) both became top performers in school and on the football field. In Greece it is common for local Greeks to sponsor foreign children and baptise them in the Greek Orthodox Church giving them Greek names. Not surprisingly, when that happened they stopped joining us for Sunday worship.

For now, during these early days of our friendship, we made quite a group. The differing languages made teaching rather a challenge but somehow we all managed to understand as I taught in English and Gill translated into Greek. There was Vera, Elkioni and Irini, who were Albanians speaking Greek; there was Gill from Wales and her two boys, plus her Greek mother-in-law; English Françoise was married to a Greek and they had two boys who both spoke English, but only Ben, the eldest, spoke Greek as well After the singing, the children would sit in the dining room with felt-tip pens and draw pictures of whichever Bible story we had told, which gave some Bible theme to plant in their fertile young minds. It wasn't exactly Sunday school, or ideal, but it was all we could manage at that stage with our limited resources. Later on, things would improve.

It wasn't only on Sundays, or visits to Irini, Eros and Elkioni, that demonstrated the increasingly major part of my life that children were becoming. I had accepted an offer to teach English to two Greek children, who were four and six years old. The idea was to teach them English through play while their parents were working. Having had almost no contact with children in my life in England, this was a whole new experience. It was therefore quite a surprise to me to find myself becoming rather fond of the little girl, who behaved like an angel most of the time. Her brother was a different story and it was quite a challenge to keep his attention for an hour. It certainly opened my eyes to the difficulties that young parents face when children enter their lives. Nevertheless, for the Barbara that in my pre-Christian days had no time for children at all, this was a major change of heart. I even found myself wondering if perhaps it wasn't too late to have children of my own after all.

The summer passed, the tourists started to thin out considerably and we waited longingly for the first of the autumn rains to soak the thirsty, dusty fields, where there was now not a blade of grass to be seen. It was on that very day of the first autumn rain that our friends, who pastored the Lighthouse Church in Piraeus, came for a holiday on Paros. Always a sign of blessing, the rain which greeted their arrival seemed to somehow foreshadow the outpouring of the Holy Spirit that they would bring with them and which would flow out to us.

The circumstances of their decision to come to Paros were nothing short of miraculous. As they lived in the Athenian port of Piraeus with their three children, we were not expecting a visit from them, especially not over a weekend because they led the Sunday meetings in the Lighthouse Church. The story unfolded that Wayne had been to a lunch where he met the vicar of Saint Andrew's Church in Athens. In conversation, the vicar mentioned that a couple living on Paros had offered their house free of charge to any missionaries who would like to use it for a holiday. Even knowing that Peter and I were here on the island he still didn't feel inclined to take up the offer, yet he found himself repeatedly thinking about it. He decided that he might as well ask for the details even if he then decided not to accept. A fax duly arrived and Wayne was more than a little surprised to see my husband named as the person who would call by the house to ensure everything was in order. Perhaps God was leading them to come to Paros by providing them with a luxury villa free of charge during their stay here. They certainly worked hard enough leading the church all year round to deserve some holidays.

Throughout their stay we had several meetings at their villa and at our house, with people of quite a variety of nationalities joining us. We still had the Kenyan ladies as well as Gill coming to us on Sundays; Adrienne comfortably translated into Greek for Yannis and Vera, so they could be a part of it all.

South African Tony joined us for the midweek meetings since he worked evenings and weekends. It was on one such mid-week meeting after a pleasant spaghetti meal together that we were praying for a fresh anointing. Peter spoke in a tongue quite unlike his more normal prayer tongue and the whole experience was quite profound. We were so excited about the things happening that we were all back at 11a.m. the next day for more of the presence of God.

Nevertheless, we had to live in the real world with ordinary people who couldn't yet share or understand any of what we were enjoying in the presence of God. An English lady, Jane, had arrived the week before Wayne and Adrienne and had pitched her tent in our garden under the kitchen window. Each year she was able to save enough money for the flight to Greece, food and spending money for two weeks, but the cost of accommodation was beyond her budget. Pitching her tent with us and having some place so close to the beach was just perfect for her. The first year that she came to camp with us we hardly knew her at all, but after several summers "*chez* Logaras" we began to know her quite well and understand some of her past difficulties. People like Jane were never going to find God while we were all sitting in our holy huddle. Taking her a cup of tea every morning and enjoying meals on our terrace together were better steps to sharing our love and friendship.

The anointing that we had been seeking in our meetings still continued to be very evident during these weeks. One Monday evening I was in the kitchen preparing food when the anointing fell upon me. I started to laugh and then laughed and laughed with such joy until my sides ached! I literally danced for joy. It was like being completely drunk without a drop of alcohol!

When Wayne and Adrienne called by later that evening and I told them what had happened, that was all it took to start Adrienne off. This was infectious! It was something that I could see would be hard for some Christians to understand, let alone non-Christians; here it was happening just on the day that Peter's mum and his sister Marie Rose were arriving. Well, in for a penny, in for a pound. Two days after they arrived we had another morning meeting and Mum and Marie Rose decided to come. There was Peter's mum laughing her head off!

Would I be able to continue sharing this anointing of joy with others in this same way, after Wayne and Adrienne had left?

Things were to take a surprising turn and, after those early years of ministering to adults of all nationalities, it seemed God had a plan for the children of Paros.

3 THE CHILDREN

For more than a year, we had a few English and Albanian children coming to our house on Sundays with one or both parents. The children would draw and look at their story books and illustrated Bibles in the dining room while we sang and listened to teaching cassettes in the lounge. With such a small house church, it didn't seem practical to try to run a Sunday school during the adults' meeting. However, with the arrival of an English missionary couple on the island for a few months, perhaps we could arrange something. Mike and Gill, the new couple, would be able to provide some input to the adult meeting while I concentrated on teaching the children.

For the four Sundays in December we invited some additional local children and read the Christmas Story; we made a simple crib, angels and stars, which all helped to bring out the real meaning of Christmas for them.

They enjoyed it so much that, as 1996 turned into 1997, we decided to continue the Christmas Sunday school into the New Year. It went really well. We started with the basics of the Christian faith praying each week for practical ideas on how to present it to the children in an interesting way.

Annamarie, a Swiss Christian living on the far side of the island near the main town, had joined us a few months earlier. Living near her were two English families who both had young girls – Jodie, aged five and Laura, aged six. They decided they would like to come so Annamarie faithfully drove them over each week. She became a link to an ever increasing circle of foreigners in Parikia as well as a close friend.

All of the children except Albanian Irini spoke English and, because most of the books we had were from England, that became the language for our lessons. This meant that I needed to give Irini English lessons during the week. Hopefully, it would help her later at school and in the meantime would enable her to follow on Sundays. Since none of the children could read or write English we needed to teach them.

Our repertoire of children's songs became extensive and by the following Christmas we were ready to try our second Nativity play. Annamarie made a beautiful wooden crib with 'off-cuts' from the local carpenter and we made the costumes together. The English mothers, the visiting grandmothers, plus a few friends made a happy gathering as the children re-enacted the story of the shepherds visiting Mary, Joseph and baby Jesus. We sang Christmas carols and later on shared pizza and traditional English mince pies. I wondered what would have to happen to make the parents want to come every Sunday instead of just for special occasions.

I was cautious about trying to lead such young children to the decision to receive Jesus into their lives, not wanting them to make a premature commitment that they didn't fully understand. I felt obliged to impress upon them very early on that they were not Christians just because they came to Sunday school. To become a Christian, I taught them that they would very simply have to say the following:

1. THANK YOU Jesus for dying on the cross for my sins.

2. SORRY for all the wrongs things I have done.

3. ASK Jesus the Son of God to come into my heart forever.

4. I RECEIVE YOU Jesus as my Lord and Saviour. AMEN.

I explained that some people would want to do this when they were quite young, while others would not understand until they were much older, maybe 18, 20 or 30 years old. For some people it could even be as late as the age of 50 or 60. Tragically, there were those who would never understand and for them it would be too late!

It became quite difficult to hold the children back. "But I love Jesus, I believe He's the Son of God, I want to follow Jesus", they chorused! In the end, it seemed best to leave it in God's hands. Those who wanted to say the prayer did; others said they didn't think they understood and that was all right, too. For those who did pray to receive Christ, following through with a believer's baptism was a hurdle yet to overcome. Having been refused when I asked the first child's father, I left it to God to move their non-Christian parents to give their permission. The parents would eventually see whether their child's commitment was genuine.

For the time being our work seemed to be with the children so Peter, Annamarie and I gave ourselves over to them. We changed the emphasis on Sundays to that of a children's church, although we were able to accommodate the occasional adult visitors.

4 A MIRACULOUS JOURNEY

During the summer of '97, it became increasingly difficult to be the owner of a vehicle without Greek number plates. For years, it had been notoriously expensive to buy cars in Greece: the import duties were prohibitive in order to dissuade Greeks from buying cars more cheaply abroad.

One afternoon in June the phone rang; our English friend, Barry, told us that we may need to sell our British registered cars. Although I had always been able to insure the Land Rover, I had never been able to tax the car annually, simply because it didn't have Greek number plates. As far as we were aware, there was no procedure to issue road tax to non-Greek registered vehicles.

Two days after the phone call we heard that Customs officers were making checks on all foreign vehicles and suddenly, foreign cars that had been in the country for more than six months were illegal! We decided that the best thing to do was to stop driving the Land Rover until we had more information, so Peter started using his moped to pick up Ben for Sunday school.

In the following days praying about the Land Rover, I became very aware of the passage in Romans about submitting to the government authorities, "Everyone must submit to the governing authorities, for there is no authority except that which God has established" Romans 13:1.

I also noted in my diary, "No matter how insignificant God's instructions may seem to you right now, take them seriously. What may seem of little consequence now may cause you serious consequences later." I began to think about selling the vehicle, since I no longer needed to have a vehicle that I could live in.

Around the same time I noted that there was a Christian Conference being held in England on 25 August. Kenneth and Gloria Copeland would be at the Birmingham National Exhibition Centre (NEC). I wondered if returning the Land Rover to England to sell it could somehow link in with a visit to these meetings.

July came and I was sure that this was what I was supposed to do, yet when a local garage offered to buy the vehicle for two million drachmas, I was very tempted to take the offer and spare myself the expense and difficulty of a journey to England. Two million drachmas was a little over £4,000, so it would be rather less than the £5,000 I had hoped for, but I would avoid the cost of the trip to England. However, when the garage owner made enquiries regarding the tax he would have to pay above the purchase price, he discovered it would be an additional six million drachmas!! Obviously, this was quite ridiculous and so the idea was dropped. God has His ways of getting us where he wants us.

The best course of action seemed to be to drive the Land Rover over to England and to sell it in three weeks, so minimizing the time that I would be away from Peter and our Sunday meetings. I booked the car onto the *Ariadne,* the night ferry to Piraeus, leaving Paros at 1:30a.m. on 6 August. Without God, such a journey alone would have been an impossible task.

I would have to make the journey alone because Peter

had to go to hospital in Athens to have his kidneys checked in mid-July. He was also having serious problems with his heart and we had yet to see the evidence of the healing we were praying for. He was working full-time building concrete frames for houses and it would not be easy for him to take three weeks off for a trip to England.

My schedule allowed one week for the trip across Europe to England, calling at Peter's mum in Belgium en route. I felt that when I arrived in England it would be better to try and sell the Land Rover in the London area, thus targeting the highest population. I planned to advertise it in *Exchange and Mart*, a newspaper renowned for successful car sales. It also seemed easier to take the Land Rover to the area where I had lived, north of London, to get its Ministry of Transport (M.O.T.) road test certificate since I knew where to find a garage. When I had obtained that certificate, I could then obtain the road tax disc at the car at a local post office. If I placed the advert by 14 August, it would appear in the newspaper the following week. I would have just two days to do all this as long as I arrived early Tuesday. This would give me a mere one week to sell it. I was definitely going to need God's help to for all this to work out.

In an ideal world, with the Christian Conference in Birmingham on 25 August, I would sell the Land Rover before that date yet still have the use of it to drive to Birmingham and to sleep in it during the conference. It was a lot to ask since most people would want possession of the vehicle as soon as they had bought it. I would just have to trust that, with God's help, everything would go according to plan and I would be able to fly back at the end of the three weeks. My prayer to God went something like this:

"God, if it is Your plan and Your will that I sell the Land Rover at this time, will You please:

1) Get me safely to England even though I am travelling alone.

2) Show me the route and keep the vehicle from accidents and breakdowns.

3) Let the Land Rover pass its test and obtain the road tax.

4) Help me to place the advertisement in the newspaper.

5) Send me a buyer who will pay £5000 and let me use the car for another week.

6) Let the buyer live near Heathrow or Gatwick airport so that I can deliver the car easily and not have far to go for my flight home to Greece."

It was a bit of a tall order, but I have always believed that God wants us to be specific in our prayers and that we can ask Him to help us with every detail of our life.

On the morning of 5 August I wrote in my diary: "If you remain in me and my words remain in you, ask whatever you wish, and it will be given to you" John 15:7.

And so it was that, on that evening, I set off from Paros to cross Europe alone. The ship, the *Ariadne*, glided into the harbour of Paros just before 1:30a.m. and, like a silent alligator, swallowed its passengers and cargo and launched into the night. I was in God's hands for the long journey ahead and the sale of the Land Rover.

The day dawned brightly as we approached Piraeus, the main harbour located just outside Athens. The first red glow of dawn appeared over the grimy tower blocks of Piraeus before the burning heat of another day of frantic comings and goings began. On disembarking, I turned to the right past the metro station and followed the signs for Corinth. I then took the road across the north of the Peloponnese and planned to break the journey at a pretty campsite on the coast. The ship to Italy would not leave Patras until that evening, so I had the whole day just to make the four-hour journey. I had marked a campsite along the route to eat and rest after travelling on the ship all night.

As planned, I arrived at Akrata around mid-morning but, being the peak August holiday, the campsite was full. There was nothing to do but press on and find another campsite, so I tried one at Trapezas. There I ate some feta cheese, juicy tomatoes and fresh bread from the bakery, before sleeping until 2p.m. After another two hours lying on the bed in the back of the Land Rover, quietly reading my Bible, I was suitably refreshed and continued the journey on to the port of Patras.

By 7:30p.m. I had cleared the customs house with all the usual shouting, stamping of passports and Greek bureaucracy. I boarded the ship, found my shared cabin and looked forward to meeting whoever God had chosen as my travelling companions. They turned out to be Danielle, a German lady travelling with a tour group of thirty other people, two Greek ladies and one Swiss lady who was part of a family of Christians.

The Swiss family were clearly sent by God to get me on the right route through Switzerland after I left Italy. I had planned to use the Saint Gotthard pass, but they strongly advised me against it as it was extremely congested at that time of year. They were travelling to Bern by another route using the Simplon Pass and they gave me all the details, so saving me many hours of traffic jams in dark tunnels under the Alps.

In my new life in Greece I had learnt to be very economical with my choice of food and any meals in restaurants, a marked contrast to the heydays in London. I decided that it was time to break the routine of cheese or tuna with bread and tomatoes. The self- service lunch menu included some smoked trout from the First Class Hors-d'oeuvres menu but at a very much reduced price. This was quite a gourmet treat after years in Greece and it made a fine main course for me. Later, in the evening, I dined in style on pork and mushrooms followed by a delicious cheese plate. It would be a long trip across Europe and I wasn't planning to stop at hotels or restaurants *en route*. The Land Rover fridge was well stocked and I had tins of every kind in the compact, built-in storage units.

I spoke to the two Swiss girls about Jesus but they weren't interested: a simple tract in German was as much as they would accept. Later, Danielle returned to the cabin just as I was praying to find her, since I had been unsuccessful earlier in the evening. I shared the gospel with her and we spoke about the return of Christ. Like so many others I have met, she spoke of creation as nature rather than God and said that if Jesus was real, she thought He would take everyone with Him at His return. However, that is not what He taught. Instead He said that one would be taken and one would be left. By 11p.m. it was quite late enough and, with the long drive ahead the next day, we settled down to sleep.

The approach to Venice was breathtaking. The ship seemed to literally float above Saint Mark's square and all the classical architecture. We were so close that we could see the people sitting at their tables drinking their rather expensive cups of coffee! As I disembarked I longed to follow the signs for the parking areas and to tour Venice, but I didn't dare: Italy is well known for its Mafia, thieves and high crime rate and it was not the place to leave the jeep unattended. If the Land Rover were to be stolen before my return, I would be stranded without transport and £5,000 out of pocket! The Muslim advice to "Lock up your camel" came to mind. Anyway, it was really a place I would want to share with Peter if we should ever have the chance.

I trundled along the Italian motorways at a steady 100Km/Hour (about 60 mph) in the direction of Switzerland. As evening approached, Lake Maggiore was on the sign posts and I remembered that Mum and Dad had had some marvellous holidays by the Italian lakes. It seemed a good place to turn off and find somewhere to park for the night. I couldn't have chosen a better spot;

there was a campsite right by the lake. Within minutes I was parked and swimming in the sunset with the splendour of the Italian Alps towering above me. Later, the moon shone across the still water as I spoke to a group of people camped next to me. They were Belgians so just the mention of having a Belgian husband from Leuven was enough to open up an invitation for me to join them. In just fifteen minutes over a coffee I was able to give them Flemish New Testaments and tracts, talk of the Baptism of the Holy Spirit and explain the power of Jesus to heal and to save. The tracts included more information on salvation. What a positively splendid place to fall asleep that night, safe and fulfilled.

By 9a.m. the next morning I was ready to leave. As I climbed the Swiss mountains the Land Rover seemed slower and heavier than ever, belching the occasional puff of black exhaust fumes as it chugged up the steep slopes. Checking the engine oil seemed like a good idea and, much to my relief, after a good top up the problem was solved.

Next I had to tackle the Simplon Pass and then the Simplon tunnel where the Land Rover was loaded onto a train. All the drivers and passengers remained sitting in their cars as we then sped through the seemingly endless tunnel. At 20 Km in length, it was the longest rail tunnel in the world at that time. It was a strange and unnerving experience to be in the driver's seat, speeding along and yet totally out of control! My foot automatically kept moving towards the brake, but to no avail as only the train driver himself was able to control our speed as we hurtled along.

Somehow, in that one day, I did the complete trip across Europe; Bern, Basle, Strasbourg, Metz, Luxembourg. By 9p.m. I was more than tired enough and wanted to stop for the night, but I felt no peace about sleeping alone at a motorway service area and so I pressed on. As my eyes scanned the motorway exits in Belgium looking for Leuven, I saw Louvain and thought that must be it, Peter's home town. I guessed that "Louvain" was the French spelling of the Flemish name, "Leuven". It was, but it was several exits too soon to make sense of the directions that Peter had given me on how to get from the motorway to his mum's house in the centre of town. It was glaringly evident that I was hopelessly lost and it was very late to find people to ask for directions.

First, I was on a country road through open farmland, so that wasn't right. Seeing a farm fully lit at almost midnight, it seemed wise to stop and ask for directions. The French speaking farmers were most amused at my schoolgirl French.

"Où est la route pour Leuven?" (Where is the route for Leuven?)

"Leuven, Louvain, Leuven, Louvain", they joked, and then pointed further down the road.

Finally, I approached the town and fed into the circular road: "Now what?"

My directions were useless. How would I ever find Peter's mum's house in this vast university town of narrow streets and beautiful old buildings with so many one way streets and no entry signs?!

"Oh God, Help! I'm lost!"

A young couple appeared, so I stopped to ask them directions. Although they were Hungarian, they spoke English. Then they saw my Ichthus fish on the back door and asked: "Are you a Christian? So are we, praise God! Are you lost? We can show you the way, but it's difficult from here so we'd better come with you."

So, at midnight, an unknown couple climbed into the jeep and I could only trust that God had sent them. Within no time we were approaching Tessenstraat and everything looked familiar! I thanked them very much and, with hugs and kisses, they left to seek their own way home. I wondered whether they were actually people or angels!

I felt pretty awful waking Peter's mother at that time of night, but I knew she would be upset with me if I slept in the car outside her block of flats. Besides, the use of a toilet would be very welcome! She greeted me with a big hug; she was so pleased to see me and to know that I was safe. No doubt we both slept better that night for seeing each other.

Belgium dawned hot and glorious the next day, a welcome 31C. Since the family had planned for us to spend the day together, it was perfect for a barbecue at Peter's youngest sister's house. Her husband, Jan, had built a beautiful modern open-plan house out in the country. It was in the same village of Tildonk where Peter had lived. With a huge garden, lawns bordered with roses, a vegetable plot and an area with fruit trees, it made a wonderful place to relax and enjoy the company of some of Peter's very large family. He had four sisters and all of them had children, many of whom had children of their own. On that day, Mum and I were with Chris and Jan and their two children, Wilhelm aged eleven and Helene aged nine. What a pity Peter hadn't been able to come with me. It was so nice to really feel part of the family.

The next day, after meeting some of Mum's friends, I had to leave to continue my journey to England. It was 230 miles to Calais so I left Leuven at 5p.m. in order to arrive at Calais around 8p.m. It was a simple, well signposted journey and a quick, efficient boarding procedure onto the ferry to cross the English Channel. By 10p.m. I was already in Dover but decided not to overnight there. Instead, like a pigeon returning to its loft, I headed for my previous home village of Datchworth. The M20 and M25 motorways would be much clearer and allow an easier drive at night than if I slept overnight and waited until the morning. Although England was no longer my home, I was keen to see the village where I had lived for so many years.

It was just after midnight when I arrived in the village. I hoped to visit a couple I knew from my computer days, who still lived there in one of the large, detached houses around the village green. As I pulled up, I saw that the house was in darkness. Ah well, I supposed they had gone to bed, but it seemed odd that the car wasn't in the drive. Yes, of course they had a garage, but I knew they usually left the car in the drive. I decided to park in the drive and go to sleep. If they were at home they would wake me up in the morning. I woke very early, then drifted off again and finally woke with a start at 9a.m. The cooing of the doves in the English countryside perfectly complemented my feelings of contentment and tranquillity.

It was obvious that my friends weren't at home. All that I could do was to leave a note saying that I had called by. Now that it was daylight, I could set about finding very special friends of mine, my ex-next door neighbours. After I had left for Greece they had moved to another village just a mile or so down the road, but I had never been to their new house. Nine o'clock in the morning seemed a better time to risk knocking on the wrong door than midnight! I found their house tucked in the corner of a wooded cul-de-sac of houses, an area that I hadn't previously explored. Mo opened the door and the sheer delight in seeing each other again after so many years was mutual. It was our first reunion since I had left with Peter in 1992, five whole years earlier and their daughter Christina was now eleven, so there was a huge change from the little six year old I'd last seen.

The plan was that I would stay with Mo and Gareth for a few days while I obtained the road test certificate needed to sell the Land Rover. I would place an advert in *Exchange and Mart*, the newspaper most well known for buying and selling anything second hand, and especially cars. First, I needed to get it through its M.O.T. (Ministry of Transport) road test. The first time around it failed! The suspension struts needed replacing after years of bouncing around on Greek island roads and dirt tracks. In addition, the rear red light covers were badly faded from all that Greek sunshine and I needed new ones. So, it was off to a garage in

Whitwell, a nearby tiny country village, to leave it to be repaired. They assured me it would be ready the next day.

In the meantime, we could enjoy fine English steaks barbecued in the garden. It was wonderful to relax together; we had been such good friends in the years before I left for Greece. Later in the day, it was a special privilege to read a bedtime story to my goddaughter, Christina. As I sat looking at her beautifully furnished and co-ordinated bedroom, with the sun and moon on the deep blue curtains, a matching quilt, cuddly bears and rabbits, I thought of some of the Albanian children on Paros. What a contrast! How very blessed the people of Northern Europe are by comparison.

Happily, the Land Rover passed the M.O.T. after the garage had carried out the repairs at a cost of £220. If only the man at our local Paros garage had identified the problems and repaired them, it would have been a lot cheaper and easier to fix there. Ah, well! The next hurdle to overcome was that I discovered you can't tax a car which has non-English insurance. The lady at the post office remained impervious to my protestation of: "We are in Europe now; it's all supposed to be one Europe."

There was nothing to do but take a minimum period insurance cover with an English company and return to the Post office waving my English insurance documents. That required a trip to the largest nearby town, Welwyn Garden City, and another £55 insurance plus £78 road tax, all just to have the required paperwork in order to sell the car.

The advert was placed in the newspaper:
LAND ROVER 1986
110 DIESEL 2.5 £5000
Overland Safari fitted bed, cupboards, fridge and shower
Mileage 62,000 and a one year M.O.T. certificate.

I put Mo and Gareth's phone number in the advert

because Gareth was a great salesman to take any calls.

Once that was done, I was ready to depart to Harrogate to visit Mum and Dad for my mum's birthday. It was a quick four-hour drive to Harrogate, a beautiful old English Cotton Mill town which had become fashionably elegant in latter years and quite a Business Centre for conferences. I found Mum and Dad's apartment easily. Gosh, it was good to see them again; I had been away a long time.

We ate a perfect English tea – honey melon, then a ham salad followed by strawberries and cream. Somehow, when I was in Greece surrounded by all that God was doing there, I could push to the back of my mind how much I missed them and not even really think about it that much. Here, surrounded by familiar photographs, everything that used to be home came flooding back to me. Dad came down to the visitor's guest room in the apartments which they had booked for me. We hugged and he told me how much they missed me, especially as they got older. I realised what a sacrifice we had all made for the sake of the gospel; my giving up being close to them, my family, my friends and my country. I was reminded of the Bible verse: "Anyone who has left home, or wife, or brothers, or parents, or children for the sake of the kingdom of God, will not fail to receive many times as much in this age and in the age to come, eternal life". Yes, it was true, I had been rewarded with a husband, a home, a second mum (Peter's mum), and also John and Barbara, an older couple on Paros, who were like a mother and father to me. I also had four new sisters (Peter's sisters), plus many nieces and nephews, new friends, as well as food and clothes in abundance. All that I had left behind I had been given afresh but, for Mum and Dad, life just went on as before but with their daughter over a thousand miles away.

We spent the days together in Harrogate and made visits to nearby classical country sites like Ripley Castle. I also was able to fit in a visit to the Christian bookshop and, as always, I came away loaded with books.

By Wednesday, I had received a call from a young man in Horsham, Sussex, who wanted to buy the Land Rover. I fell to my knees and thanked God not only for finding a buyer but also for not leaving it until the very last minute. I would drive back to Welwyn for him to come and view the vehicle.

On my last day in Harrogate, Dad and I went to visit a neighbour that Dad played snooker with. He was having trouble with his hips and had difficulty in walking. Knowing how successful prayers for healing from prostate cancer had been for my dad, Bob was keen to do all he could to receive his healing for his hips. I started to explain that healing in Jesus' name went hand in hand with salvation in Jesus' name. After all, it would be tragic to receive a healing to one's body in this life and then spend all eternity separated from God because of a failure to receive Christ's free offer of salvation. We prayed with him to receive Christ, praying for his healing as we laid hands on him in Jesus' name and left. Just two days later, Dad phoned to say that Bob had got out of bed with no pain and walked without his sticks. What a faithful God we serve!

Alan, the young man interested in buying the Land Rover, arrived in Welwyn as arranged. He was looking for a vehicle to take on safari to Africa, as his own, which he had prepared for the trip, had been stolen. Understandably, he loved mine but wanted to haggle a bit over the price. I was never very good at bargaining and when he asked if I would I take £4,750, I foolishly agreed, knowing that it was easily worth £5000, especially with all the extra brand-new spare parts it had with it for desert breakdowns.

Exactly as I had prayed, God had brought the buyer in the time frame I had asked for, he lived near Gatwick airport for my return flight home, and he was even willing to let me have the use of it for one more week to go to the Christian Conference in Birmingham. Oh, why did I cave in and let him have it for £4,750 when I had asked God for £5,000? Oh well, another lesson learnt, just as with the purchase of the land on Paros. God had told me the price to pay, £30,000, yet under pressure from the seller I had given in and paid 25 percent more. It was obvious I would never make a saleswoman!

Alan was off to Devon for a long weekend surfing. He was happy to delay the full payment for a week and just give me the £200 deposit he had with him, plus his address in order for me to deliver the vehicle the following Saturday. He would then pay me the balance and drive me to Gatwick or Heathrow airport when I had found a flight. Now I could drive to my old church in Stevenage that Sunday and continue up to Birmingham on Monday for the conference. I planned to sleep in the Land Rover on a campsite, which would save a fortune on hotels in the Birmingham area.

I started to look for a flight home at a sensible price. I spent Saturday phoning adverts from the *London Evening Standard* newspaper for flights to Athens. In those days, the Internet hadn't taken off and it wasn't as easy then as it is now to book flights. I finally settled on a Virgin Atlantic flight from Heathrow on the following Saturday evening. Little did I know that, while I was at the conference for six days, God would show me the make and model of car to replace the Land Rover.

The conference turned out not to be at the Birmingham National Exhibition Centre, as I had understood, so the campsite I had chosen was miles from the actual central Birmingham location of the conference. When I finally found the conference location and pulled into the multi-storey car park, it seemed as good a place as any to sleep at night. The evening sessions finished quite late around 10p.m. Why drive miles out of the centre of Birmingham, unsure of the way, when I could settle down there, pull the curtains and be asleep within half an hour of the session ending? It wasn't very pretty with concrete pillars, floors and ceilings with a maze of pipes and conduits but who cared, I hadn't come for the view! Besides, there were security guards on duty all night, plus my guardian angel, so I couldn't be safer. This decided, I had unknowingly also decided that the Land Rover would sit in the same parking bay for the whole conference. Due to the generally low ceilings and the extra height of the Land Rover with the roof rack on top, I found myself parked next to a man with a higher than usual Subaru.

In spite of its tiny size from the outside, his Subaru was a seven-seater. It was a bit like the Tardis! On the last day of the conference, for no apparent reason, the man said, "Would you like me to show you around my car?" Why not? He showed me how the back seats folded forward to make it like a van to allow all kinds of things to be transported. The front seats all folded flat to make a bed, rather like the Land Rover, and it did have a four-wheel drive. Though it was missing the fridge, storage cupboards and shower of the Land Rover, it was at least more versatile than a standard, four-seater saloon. Could it be that God was showing me what kind of vehicle I needed in Greece for future requirements that I was as yet unaware of? Indeed He was, and He was about to bring it right to our door on Paros and even in the same colour, white!

The conference was like food to a hungry man. By living on-site, so to speak, I was able to attend every session except the last one on the Saturday night. I had to be down in Horsham in the afternoon with the Land Rover to be sure to get to the airport in plenty of time. I wanted to check in around 7p.m. It should have been a straightforward journey down the M1 and around the M25, but I hadn't reckoned on getting a flat tyre. The Land Rover pulled badly to the nearside and I managed to limp to the motorway service area. I had changed the wheels on many occasions so it didn't occur to me that I would have any difficulty. No matter how hard I tried, I just couldn't get the nuts off the wheel. Clearly, one garage or another had put the wheels back on with a spider wrench. There was nothing else to do but to call out a break down service as there was no help on hand at the motorway petrol station. At least they came quickly and I was back on the road, but that was another £42 in additional costs. I had three spare wheels with me, one on the door and two on the roof rack, so it was no real problem. I had deliberately allowed plenty of time for the journey.

As I turned off the M25 motorway and followed Alan's directions, I wound along the small country lanes, praying and trusting I wouldn't get lost as I now didn't have any time to spare. It was exactly 5p.m. when I pulled up at his house. Alan invited me in and had the £4,550 in cash in a large brown envelope on the table. We sat together as I counted it, and then he and his girlfriend were all set to drive me to Heathrow airport. They even parked and escorted me to the bank so I could safely deposit the money. God had not overlooked a single detail in the whole trip.

As the plane took off, I marvelled at how I had driven safely across Europe, sorted out the taxation and required paperwork to sell the Land Rover, sold it as asked to someone who lived near the airport, banked the money and flown home, all in just twenty-five days! Just how was that possible? Because I asked God to help me do it and He is an amazing God! It was yet another example of faith in Jesus not being just a ticket to heaven, but help in the here and now, in every practical detail of life. It was a fine example of the quotation: "It's not just pie in the sky when you die, but cake on the plate while you wait!"

5 A WEDDING

Safely back in Greece, it seemed it was time to add weddings to our list of church functions. We already had the Sunday school for children, Sunday meetings for adults and baptisms as required, simply because we were the only English speaking Christian group on the island.

Close friends of ours, Alan and Dorothy, had a delightful apartment in Piso Livadi, with glorious views across the harbour to the neighbouring island of Naxos. By day, Piso Livadi lay quietly dozing: a few foreign tourists sizzling in the blazing heat, visiting Greeks lounging under the trees at the back of the narrow strip of soft sand, and small children splashing around in the shallow water. By night, the whole place came alive. The people, freshly showered and revived after the heat of the day, would trickle down from surrounding rooms and villages to eat. Some would simply promenade along the picturesque little harbour strewn with yachts and fishing boats. With twinkling stars, moonlit water and the distinct strains of Greek bouzouki music wafting on the gentle breeze, it was a lover's paradise.

Alan and Dorothy's son, Stephen, and his beautiful

fiancée, Samantha, were ready to tie the knot, so why not marry on Paros in the sunshine rather than in the rain in Milton Keynes with its famous new town concrete cows! May was selected as the best month, and the nearby village of Marpissa had a town hall with a local mayor who would be able to perform the legal ceremony. Even so, with the hurdle of Greek bureaucracy and the language to overcome, they were going to need some help. This was where I came in. Much to my delight they felt that the Greek Civil Wedding vows were somewhat brief and lacking in the solemnity and commitment of an English wedding: "We are gathered here today to in the sight of God to join this man and woman in Holy matrimony . . ."

They asked if it would be possible for me to lead a short service, reading from the Bible, before the actual official Greek wedding service started. Of course I was only too happy to oblige, but never having done such a thing before, I was anxious to find something thought provoking for the guests as well as the bride and groom. I finally settled on a passage from the Old Testament, Ecclesiastes 4:9–12:

"Two are better than one, because they have a good return for their work:

If one falls down, his friend can help him up.

But pity the man who falls and has no one to help him up!

Also, if two lie down together, they will keep warm.

But how can one keep warm alone?

Though one may be overpowered, two can defend themselves.

A cord of three strands is not quickly broken."

I explained that two people coming together in a marriage was a powerful combination of their work, their companionship, the physical intimacy and their help to one another in difficult times. The secret of a strong marriage, a marriage that will stand the test of time, is the third strand, the God factor.

In Switzerland, mountain climbers are well aware the ropes that tie climbers together on the peaks and cliff faces must be strong enough to hold in life-threatening situations. It has been discovered that a rope made of three cords is infinitely stronger than a rope made of two cords and, strangely, it is even stronger than a rope made with four cords. The third cord or strand in a marriage needs to be God, entwined together with the husband and wife, binding them together even when disaster strikes and their very lives are in danger: this could be a life-threatening illness, or lesser threats such as redundancy, financial hardships and the many other challenges of life. Interestingly, the third cord of these climbing ropes is usually coloured red. Just as the rope saves a person who falls from physical death, so the red blood of Jesus saves us all from spiritual death.

It was a short message followed by the traditional English wedding vows, but it was one that I hoped Stephen and Samantha would remember for years to come. Before the official Greek wedding ceremony began, they each confirmed that they understood the solemn and binding nature of the wedding that they were about to undertake. Samantha's father, Martin, very emotionally gave his daughter's hand to Stephen as he was asked "Who gives this woman to be married to this man?" After a short blessing, the mayor entered, right on cue, just as I had finished speaking. He was better known to us as Tassos from the local hardware shop, and the wedding service was a friendly, informal affair. With the help of the prepared English translation, the extremely brief Greek civil ceremony was read. The groom was asked if he took this bride to be his wife, to which he replied yes. Then the bride was asked if she took the groom to be her husband and she gladly accepted.

The photographs taken outside Marpissa Town Hall certainly couldn't have been mistaken for an English wedding! The splendid marble cornice over the doorway of the town hall, the purple bougainvilleas and palm trees, together with the gleaming white Cycladic architecture around the village square, all made a perfect, distinctly Greek backdrop. They were also able to take some photographs in front of the beautiful, white, Greek Orthodox church across the square.

It was a happy crowd that descended the hill from the village to Anna and Giorgos' taverna to eat, drink and celebrate in true, Greek style. It promised to be a long night, something Greek weddings were famous for!

6 COLORADO

By the time 1999 rolled around, it was ten years since I had left the security of a job and a regular income. I had learnt about God's many ways of provision for food and clothes and a place to live. There had been difficult times when we had had to pray for the money for food and rent, and any kind of holiday – certainly a trip abroad – was way beyond our means. It seemed it was time for God to show me that he could enable me to travel anywhere in the world He wanted me to go, and that He could supply the airfare through anyone He chose. While this was to be the first time He would do this, it was not to be the last.

I had met Amy from Colorado on that first summer in Paros and we had kept in regular contact throughout the intervening ten years. She had visited Paros several times since that first trip and now was married to Robin and they had a daughter, Hannah. Hannah's birth was a miracle, astonishing enough to inspire anyone else who was trying unsuccessfully to conceive and give birth. Amy had miscarried seven times! The pain and heartache of losing seven babies at various stages of gestation can probably only be understood by someone who has gone through the same experience.

On a visit to Paros after her seventh miscarriage, I asked Amy if I could explain to her some relevant biblical teaching. I rather suspected that her inability to carry a child the full term had some spiritual cause and was not one of the physical causes being investigated by the gynaecologist. In the Bible, God's handbook for life, the book of Deuteronomy explains that God promises blessings for obedience to His Word. If we obey His commandments, all these blessings will come upon us; we will be blessed in the city and the country, the fruit of our womb will be blessed and our finances will be blessed. On the other hand, disobedience to His commandments can open the door to a long list of possible curses. If this only related to our own actions, it would simplify the process, but if someone disobeyed His commands, the effects could be felt by up to four generations. This means that adverse things, such as infertility, may not only be the result of our own actions, but could also result from the actions of our parents, two pairs of grand-parents and four pairs of great grand-parents. Interestingly, while curses affect four generations, God promises to bless up to a thousand generations of those who love Him.

Idolatry is not just worshipping idols of wood and metal, Buddha statues and other temple gods, but a whole myriad of things we put in the place of God, even things like astrology. Looking to the stars for guidance for our future rather than to God is also idolatry, as the prophet Isaiah makes clear. These apparently innocent activities have been revealed to be the root cause of so many problems in people's lives.

Amy and I sat down with a Bible and Derek Prince's book *Blessing or Curse, You Can Choose*. We worked through all kinds of events in her life, especially some of the things she had been into in her wilder days. She prayed for forgiveness and in the name of Jesus we broke the resulting curses over her life. The proof of the pudding was in the eating: just one year later Amy gave birth to

Hannah!

When Amy and Robin told us that they were planning a holiday on Paros with their new baby girl, we were delighted. Unfortunately, it was the year that anti-American feelings were riding high in Greece. When demonstrators burnt the American flag on the streets of Athens, Amy and Robin began to question the wisdom of a trip to Greece with a young baby. In America, the government was warning Americans not to travel to Greece until things calmed down. It was a big disappointment to us when we heard that they weren't coming, but then they offered us tickets to fly to Colorado so that we could all be together. I was delighted at the idea, but Peter couldn't begin to contemplate a transatlantic flight of more than ten hours, not to mention the additional four hours to fly to England to connect with the flight. Tickets were considerably cheaper from London to the USA than from Athens. At first, I assumed that Peter's reluctance to travel would mean that I wouldn't be able to take up the offer to travel either. On the contrary, he was more than happy for me to make the trip if I wanted to go. Naturally, I was disappointed that it would be an experience we wouldn't be able to share together, but it seemed much too great an opportunity to be passed by. Besides, I really wanted to see Amy and Robin and the miracle baby, Hannah. The thought of being able to visit their church in the Rocky Mountains, to hear them both singing in their rock gospel choir and to meet with their Christian friends, had me jumping up and down with excitement. It would be a wonderfully refreshing time for me.

It was with this background to the trip that, in November 1999, I set out from Paros to travel to Colorado via London. Since I was travelling to England, I had some other visits to make. First, I visited friends from the Milton Keynes church as it was on my way up to Harrogate to see my mum and dad. My sister, Margaret, and her daughter joined us there for the weekend and then it was off to London to visit my nephew. Next I moved on to Guildford to visit my friend Francoise, who had lived on Paros for more than ten years. Guildford was on the way to Gatwick airport, so it was not out of my way at all. Walking together in the park, the trees decked with red and golden leaves, reminded me of all the beauty of the English countryside that I had left behind. Autumn had always been my favourite time of year. How different from the pines, palms and olive trees of Paros that I had become accustomed to.

The next day I arrived early at Shalford station to travel on to Gatwick airport, Shalford being a small suburb of Guildford. Much to my horror, the train to Gatwick was cancelled! Again, I was totally dependent on God to rescue the situation or I could lose my ticket to Colorado. I explained my predicament to a fellow passenger waiting on the platform and prayed. Lo and behold, he marched along the platform to a small station telephone and spoke with the signal man. Astonishingly, they stopped the 08:21a.m. Gatwick express just for me! How do other people manage to live without a helpline to God?

The remainder of the journey went smoothly and I eventually made it to Colorado, via Minneapolis, and then on to Denver. The airport clock said it was 19:00, still early evening, but my body clock was telling me it was much later and definitely time for bed. Amy was waiting for me, and we travelled by car across the Denver plain to Boulder before climbing the winding mountain pass another 2,000 feet up to the town where they she lived. It was just like I had imagined, mountain slopes, log cabins and lots of trees! Hannah, their precious little baby girl, looked like a tiny doll. What a glorious miracle! They were a family, at last!

The next morning I was in for a big surprise; the whole place had been magically transformed overnight by the first fall of snow! I peeked out from the window above my bed: it looked like the houses were sleeping under a fluffy white blanket. The snow hung tenaciously to the heavily laden branches until, every now and then, the squirrels would run along a branch and the snow would fall to the ground like a dollop of freshly whisked meringue. Outside, the cat sat on the windowsill in rapt wonder.

There was a prayer meeting at the Calvary Chapel at 9:30a.m. Then, in the afternoon, Amy and I went for a walk with their gorgeous dog, a white Labrador. Gosh, it was cold – just 28F at night – and the air was so thin that high up, it was hard just to get enough oxygen. All the men really did look like the all-American cowboys in the films, wearing cowboy hats, leather boots and driving huge pick-up trucks.

Going out to eat was quite an experience, too. The steaks were enormous, the sour cream on the jacket potatoes delicious, and the blue cheese dressing on the salads something really special. Faint memories stirred of my life before my exile on Paros. I was just grateful to be able to experience something of how other people lived. I only had $100 dollars in my pocket for the whole trip, so it was best not to look at the prices and be grateful that Amy and Robin were paying for me.

The timing of my trip coincided with American Thanksgiving, and I was to experience a huge Thanksgiving dinner at a superb house out in the woods together with many of the people from church. It was the first time I had seen a children's Pilgrim's Play, learning the origins of the first Thanksgiving, and I just loved watching the children in their costumes and black pilgrim hats.

Other notable events of my stay included Amy's birthday, almost daily gatherings at the Chapel and a continual stream of visitors to the house. What a wonderful community life they all shared. I had never experienced anything like it, neither in England nor in Greece. There were sick friends to pray for, unsaved friends to talk to, and so many stories to listen to of changed lives as their friends had turned from pot to praise! Most of them hadn't come from Christian families or church backgrounds, and they were a wonderful testimony of God's love in the lives of ordinary people. Some of their ancestors had been involved with Spiritism, and many of the friends had been a part of the American drugs scene. These guys just loved to play guitar and sing, so at most get-togethers, someone would start singing and then the rest would join in with some well-loved choruses. Many of them were in the Calvary Chapel Gospel Choir, so the music was lively, gospel-style, handclapping choruses.

It seemed I couldn't go anywhere without the Lord leading me to those He wanted to help. One lady was greatly in need of spiritual help; I'll call her Katie. Her mother, grandmother and aunt had all had cancer and five out of six of her mother's brothers had died of cancer. Katie herself had cancer in her foot at the time of my visit. Again, it was back to the basic teaching of blessings for obedience and curses for disobedience to God's word going back through the four generations of her family. Had she been involved in occult things such as Ouija-boards, Astrology, or Tarot cards? Had there been things in the house relating to other religions such as Buddha statues, Hindu elephants, Chinese dragons or snakes? (Both are symbols of Satan in the Bible). What was her relationship with her parents? Did she honour them? "Honour your father and your mother that it may go well with you." We talked and prayed, working through the seven steps to release from a curse. Just as I had been enabled to bring this teaching on blessings and curses to this small community Colorado, so later on it would help others to find healing and release. Three years after my visit, I received a small card from Di, who had helped us with the baptisms on Paros. I still have the card to this day and it reads:

"I wanted to tell you about a small seed you planted,

that grew and blossomed this summer. When I returned from Greece (Paros), a friend of mine was suffering from depression, confusion and Fibromyalgia and general malaise. As we prayed and talked, she told me that her sister runs an American psychic institute and that her brother uses psychic ability to heal people. Her aunt also practised the witchcraft arts. I remembered the book you introduced me to, Derek Prince's *Blessing or Curse, You can Choose*. We both bought copies and committed to reading, discussing and praying, as we read through the book together all summer. She recently told me that she is better than she has ever been and she gives a lot of credit to the way the Lord used the book to reveal things to her. Thank you from me and her. It was a wonderful lesson to me about keeping an open mind when it comes to the Lord."

For me, this was a great source of encouragement. If I would simply share with others what the Lord has taught me, He would set the people free and release them from oppression, sickness, marital problems and financial problems.

As well as the ministry and spiritual side of the holiday, there were of course opportunities for a bit of sight-seeing even though Amy and Robin both had to work during my stay. One of the highlights was a trip to the National Park. It was absolutely awesome to see the majestic peaks, now capped with snow, and the elk and reindeer running free. There was mile upon mile of open space with not a house to be seen, nature at its most unspoilt. Millions upon millions of pine trees stretched out as far as the eye could see. What a contrast to the sparse scrub and neatly walled terraces of olive trees on Paros.

The days slipped by and suddenly the trip was over. It was time to leave the tranquillity of the mountains to head for the airport at Denver. We wound our way down the mountain road to Boulder, dropping down into the valley. Then it was a plane to Minneapolis, Minneapolis to Gatwick London and later on to Athens. Fortunately, I had arranged a most welcome stop-over with friends who lived near Gatwick Airport. Brian and Christine kindly met me at the airport and brought me to their elegant home. As we drove up the imposing tree-lined driveway my eyes were already closing, and it was good to be able to fall into bed and sleep for hours after the long journey. My body clock was way out of sync.

The next day, refreshed after a lovely meal and a full night's sleep, it was time to continue home to Peter and Paros.

7 THE NEW MILLENIUM

A date no one on Paros will ever forget is 26 September 2000. The weather was stormy, there was a key football match on the TV and the regular ferry was on its way down from Athens. It would normally get into the harbour on Paros just before 10p.m., but that night was to be a disaster beyond anyone's imagination. As the ferry approached Paros, the passengers probably started to descend the stairs to the lower car deck as usual. For as many years as I can remember, passengers have always gone down to the car deck just before the ship docked, to make the disembarkation procedure quicker. The ramp is usually winched down as the ship speeds across the waves and then, as it is lowered to the quay, the passengers stream off like lemmings rushing to the shore. This time, they never got that far. Outside the harbour, two large rocks called "The Doors", stick up above the surface of the water. Every captain of every ship knows they are there, but, on this particular night, the ship was to crash into them. The following excerpt from Wikipedia describes how such an awful event occurred. (Some details have been omitted):

"On the evening of Tuesday 26 September 2000, MS *Express Samina* left the port of Piraeus with 473 passengers and 61 crew members. When the ship was two nautical miles off the port of Parikia, Paros, it hit the reef called Portes (which means the doors) at 18 knots. The wind at the time was 8 Beaufort, that's very strong and very stormy. The ships stop sailing when it increases to 9 Beaufort. The ship sank near there an hour later, resulting in the deaths of 82 people from a total of 533 on board. The first responders to the distress call were fishing boats from the nearby port, followed by the port authorities and amazingly some British ships, in the area due to a NATO exercise. The fact that some of the crew did not help the passengers evacuate the sinking ferry contributed to the tragic death toll.

The crew had placed the ship on autopilot but had not left a crew member to watch the ship, even though it is standard practice for one crew member to watch the controls to avoid collisions with other vessels for example. A crew member discovered there was a problem and, at the last minute, tried to steer the ship to port but it was too late. Shortly after 10p.m. the ship struck the east face of the taller Portes pinnacle. The rocks tore a six-meter long and one-meter wide hole above the water line and then cut through the hull through the side, below the waterline, and next to the engine room. The water then destroyed the main generators, so there was no electrical power. A ship safety expert said that the damage sustained by the MS *Express Samina* would not normally sink such a ship. The ship sank because nine of the ship's eleven watertight compartment doors were open when safety laws require ship operators to close and lock the safety doors. The water spread beyond the engine room, and due to a lack of power, the operators could not remotely shut the doors. The open watertight doors were said to be the most significant aspect of the sinking.

People on the ship were not the only casualties. The

port-master of Parikia died the same night of a heart attack due to the stress of the evacuation operations. Two months later, the manager of the company, Minoan Flying Dolphins, committed suicide by jumping from his sixth-floor office window. He had been charged with criminal negligence in conjunction with this ferry disaster and had been the focus of much media attention. Several crew members, as well as representatives for the owners, were finally charged with different criminal charges, including manslaughter and negligence.

According to witnesses, the First officer had been watching a football match on television when the ship hit the rocks. He was sentenced to 19 years in prison, while the Captain received a 16-year sentence. Three crew members were sentenced to between 15 months and eight years and nine months for a series of misdemeanours that included abandoning ship without the captain's permission."

Three days after the disaster, because it was known that we had Albanian friends, we received a phone call asking if we could go to Parikia to help with some of the lost Albanians. People had lost all their papers and were in a terrible state of shock. I drove over to the port with our Albanian friend Yannis and we did our best to be of some assistance. The atmosphere in the usually cheerful town was heavy; the pain of death and lost loved ones was everywhere.

For the family and friends of the eighty-two people that died, life would never be the same. A lady in a nearby village lost her son and her grandson that day. How anyone ever recovers from a loss such as that, I don't know. Perhaps the passage of time eases the pain somewhat, but I doubt it ever stops hurting. I knew the family as they had an electrical shop in the village, and her husband had repaired my twenty-five year old sewing machine. Ever since the disaster, I think of her and her husband each time I use my sewing machine. I tried with my limited Greek to console her and told her how I had lost my fiancé after six years together, but it was nothing compared to her loss. As she could understand English, I gave her my book to read in the hope that it would help her to draw closer to God and to find the peace that only Jesus can bring. I also gave her a card with some words of consolation and a Greek New Testament, as many local people don't actually have one. Sadly, the electrical shop is closed now. As if the loss of her son and grandson wasn't tragic enough, her husband died only a few years later. Fortunately, she has a daughter and the remaining family are still living on Paros.

To the rest of us that live on the island and didn't lose close family or friends, the repercussions of that night live on. The ferries are our life-line. We need them to visit hospitals, to travel to major airports and to then fly abroad to visit family and friends, not to mention for simple trips to just visit friends in Athens. For young people at university, it is their link with home and family. Now, when the people rush down the stairs in their hurry to disembark quickly, I hang back at the top of the steps until the ship docks safely. If someone tries to hurry me along, I just say, "Remember the *Samina*! I'll wait, thank you".

It was just a few weeks after the disaster that my mum, dad and sister were booked to fly out for an October holiday. They flew to Athens Airport and then came down by ferry to Paros. I was understandably relieved when they arrived safely on Paros. Even so, I was shocked to see how old and tired Dad looked. He could hardly walk and it seemed the journey had really taken its toll. It would be his 78th birthday in a few days' time. Fortunately, after he had been with us a few days, he seemed much better and was soon enjoying the sunshine and the famous, sticky, Greek sweets; *baklava* being his favourite. Throughout the visit, I was so aware that we only had fourteen days together. One day I wrote in my diary, "I must treasure every moment of each day that we have. There are seven whole days left."

But it was over all too soon and I was on the ferry with them to go back to Athens Airport. To break up the journey, we had booked a hotel in the yachting marina in Piraeus, which is a pleasant place to spend an evening, unlike the main shipping harbour which is dirty, noisy and congested. At least we could find a pleasant restaurant for our last evening together before they took the plane. Mum and Dad were happy to order spaghetti, while Margaret and I had prawns baked in a pot in cheese and tomato sauce, called "prawns *saganaki*".

The next day I cried as I hugged the three of them goodbye. To be separated from my family was such a price to pay to preach the gospel in this nation of Greece. In the early years here, it was all so fresh and new and exciting; living on a Greek island, preaching the gospel, meeting Peter, falling in love, getting married and building the house. Yet, as the years passed, I became increasingly aware of the cost to myself and my family, how much I loved them and missed them. Yes, my dad wrote faithfully every week, and we did telephone regularly so they knew all was well, but even that had been difficult in the early years. There were no phone boxes on the streets in those days: it was way before the era of mobile phones and the only place to make a phone call was the little grocery shop in the village in the square by the main Orthodox church. Margarita ran the shop, selling fresh home-grown vegetables, fresh eggs and various tinned foods, as well as bags of sugar. It was also the place to buy all sewing and knitting materials, since that was what Greek women did to pass the time and clothe the family. Embroidery was particularly popular and the village ladies made the most beautiful tablecloths and curtains. Tucked away in a corner of the shop was a cubicle containing the public telephone. It was the only one available on this side of the island where you could make a metered call in private and pay at the end. A few other places allowed short calls on the meter, but the whole shop could hear every word you said as you hovered near the door and the checkout! Snuggled away in the cubicle at Margarita's, we could speak in relative privacy. After 1994, when we built our house on Logaras, we had the luxury of a phone of our own, but even to get that I had had to put my name on the waiting list for a phone, years before the house was ever built. I had visions of a little wooden box with a telephone in it hanging on the telegraph pole on my land, waiting for the house to be built, but of course things don't move that quickly in Greece. The house was finished long before the phone arrived. Now, we had regular contact by phone. Well, we did if other people called us. We could just about afford the monthly phone rental charge to be able to receive calls, but not the cost of making foreign calls. Things would get better as time went by.

At least Mum, Dad and Margaret seemed relaxed and happy as they left. The holiday had done them good. Little did I know that within eighteen months, my dad would have passed on to glory. Margaret, Mum and I would be left with just an aching void, without our hero. Regrettably, a few months before he died, I decided it was ridiculous keeping every letter he had ever written to me in more than ten years and, for space reasons, threw most of them away. When he did die, I was devastated. It would have been such a comfort to have had them to reread; fortunately, I had kept some.

At some point during the course of that summer of 2000, another young man had arrived on our side of the island and it seemed our paths were to cross many times over the next fifteen years. He had lived in Stockholm and was a part of the rock music scene there, playing bass guitar in a group. They had even made a record which became a big hit. Sadly, he had slipped into the drugs scene, which was all too common in the parks and cafés. When his parents died, he and his sister received their part of the inheritance, but rather than taking it as an opportunity to make a new start, he squandered it. Finally, he drifted back to Greece, a country he had lived in for a time when he was younger and where he had married a Greek girl. The marriage had lasted one week!

I never really found out what made him wander into our courtyard one summer's day, but it resulted in us spending years trying to help him sort out his problems. He joined our Sunday meetings and was glad to stay for meals afterwards and at different times during the week. Around November time he asked if he could be baptised, so Peter and I baptised him on Logaras beach. Within a week of his baptism, we found him an apartment in the village to live in, rather than the room he was renting on the beach. For some weeks, he had adopted a local stray dog and they had become quite fond of one another. He planned to take it with him since the apartment did have a small garden where he could keep a dog. It is not hard to imagine the distress he suffered when the dog returned in terrible pain, the day he was ready to move, first vomiting and finally collapsing. Some locals had put a bowl of food out for him containing poison. I knew afterwards who it was because, earlier the same day, I had seen them mixing something, laughing together and saying that should be nice and tasty. Not being aware that anyone would even think of poisoning a dog, I had walked on without realising what they were doing. Later, having watched the dog die a most agonising, painful death, I realised what they had done. It was the first time I had seen such cruelty used to protect sheep from stray dogs. His dog had never been seen near sheep as he was buying tins of dog food to feed it out of what little money he had. While he was pleased to have a place to live that he could call home, the loss of his dog on the same day did rather put a damper on things. Poison is a daily hazard for all stray cats and dogs on the islands and is considered a practical way to cull the stray population. Even for the owners of pet cats and dogs, if an animal should wander off for a few days, the poison hazard is never far from their mind, and it is always a relief when their pet returns home safely, as we knew from our first dog, Abee.

Over the months that followed he found work in a variety of places in the local area. It was mostly gardening, something he didn't like that much, but people were kind and often fed him as well as paying him. One Greek lady was particularly good to him. When she later died of cancer, it was as if he had lost his own mother; he was grief-stricken. Happily, with the passage of time, things improved for him. He learnt the principle of giving back to God a part of what he earned, and he saw that sometimes he would quickly be offered more work, as happened with some neighbours who wanted help to pick their olives. The pinnacle of his success, job-wise, was when he obtained a regular job and earned daily insurance stamps for more than a year. This success then provided the money for him to pursue his passion with music. He had been a disc jockey in Sweden and was keen to try again to obtain work with a radio station. Once a week during the summer months, he had his own hour of 60's era music with disc jockey style chit-chat in English. He had set up a music studio in his apartment with several CD players, amplifiers and good speakers. His program was generally popular and all went well until the man who employed him had an unexpected heart attack and died young. That was the end of his short career as a radio station disc jockey. The man's wife didn't share her husband's enthusiasm for his weekly program and decided not to continue.

In later years when God had blessed him so much that he had work, money in the bank and all his bills paid, he chose to drift away from God. For several years he stopped coming to church. He said that he didn't believe any more that Jesus was the Son of God and was interested in some New Age teaching. He thereby cut himself off from the source of his blessings and by 2013 he had lost his job, his savings and his home. Fortunately, he knew what to do to put things right. He finally came to his senses and he returned to worshipping God and seeking God's help. It literally saved his life. Like many other unemployed people in Greece, he had begun to spiral downwards into a pit of depression and poverty, turning to *suma* to console himself. *Suma* is the 40% white spirit made from grape skins after the grapes have been pressed; it is also called *tsipouro*. On the island it is home-made and widely available by the litre at a very low cost. The *suma* had quite a hold on him and he needed somewhere to go to get free from the addiction. He also needed something to do and to give him hope for the future. He had always wanted to help those in need so, with the help of a ministry in Athens, just before Christmas 2014, he was able to go and join their rehab program for drug addicts and alcoholics. He would also work with the team helping homeless people on the streets of Athens. It was perfect for him, as he could relate to the drug addicts and alcoholics. He spoke fluent Greek, and his expertise with sound and music equipment was something they needed continually in setting up music presentations on the streets and at the church. He also helped at the centre where they fed the homeless several days a week.

Although we didn't have quite the same problem of homeless people on Paros, there were plenty of immigrants from outside the European Union who had come in search of work and a better life. Finding work around the year 2000 was not so difficult: there were rooms to be cleaned providing work for the women, and the building industry was booming, providing work for the men. Albanians were particular good at building the stone walls so common on Paros and it had become a bit of a dying trade with the younger locals. The older Parian men and farmers were able to do it, but their sons were more interested in studying at university than in learning how to build stone walls or milk goats! The wages they received were not that wonderful. After paying the rent, buying the food and paying the water and electricity bills, there wasn't usually much money left over to buy clothes. This was something we realized we could help them with.

For years, God had fulfilled his promise to clothe me as he did "the lilies of the fields" and had provided me with a constant supply of fabulous clothes. It was just as well, since we had neither much money for clothes and household linens, nor shops to buy them in. Most of the local ladies did their shopping in the marvellous street markets in Athens, an opportunity which rarely presented itself for me. Fortunately, there were many western European people living on the island making regular shopping trips to the UK, France, Germany and Switzerland. On their return they were faced with the problem of insufficient wardrobe space. The problem is exacerbated by the wide variations in temperature we experience between summer and winter. In the summer, we run around in shorts and sleeveless T-shirts because even a sleeve is too hot for the 30–35C temperatures; in winter, we need woollen sweaters and thermal underwear for the cold, 3–14C and the extreme humidity. The solution to the storage problem is to have upper and lower wardrobes, with a grand change over twice a year around April and late October. Up with the summer clothes, down with the warm jackets and woolly hats, then six months later, down come all the shorts and swimming costumes again. This provides a perfect opportunity for giving away anything that has become a size too small or has been replaced by something new. At first, people were sending bags to us, thinking that the clothes or bedding would be useful for us, which it was. Then, with the passage of time, we had so many clothes we needed to pass them onto others. The more it became known that we were giving clothes to Albanian families and other foreigners on the island, the more people started to send us all kinds of men's, women's and children's clothes. Many were as good as new and there was a variety of toys and household items to go with them. I had many families which I visited, so it was ideal to be able to help them practically, as well as to help with their spiritual needs by giving them New Testaments in their own language.

More and more, our house became cluttered up with bags of clothes waiting to be sorted, sometimes needing washing, and then to be delivered. I was probably the only person on Paros that had lists of the shoe sizes of whole families, as well as their names! Finally, we decided that we really needed some extra storage, but where and how?

We were surrounded by farmers who randomly erected chicken houses and stables for the sheep and goats, either close to or adjacent to their houses. A rough, concrete floor supported a simple building of grey cement blocks and then a roof could be made with wooden beams and bamboo. A screed of concrete on the top, not too heavy, would then make it rain-proof to keep animals and hay bales dry in the winter months. We decided that, while we didn't have chickens, sheep or goats, something similar would be perfect for storing bags of clothes for distribution, as well as boxes of books and tracts and Peter's tools, which could no longer all fit in the house. Since everything could be plastered white, it might even look rather nice joined to the courtyard wall next to the olive grove. Having a husband who is a builder makes such a project relatively easy, not to mention considerably cheaper than employing builders and electricians.

And so it came about that, during the winter of 2000–2001, we built what came to be known as our West Wing. It was only years later that we learnt there was a TV series of the same name, based on the American White House. By this time we had been given a cement mixer. Peter had built the whole original house by mixing the cement for the brickwork by hand, but now things would be easier. John and Barbara, our English friends, had decided that the mixer was taking up too much room in their garage and they knew that it would be a big help to Peter. It was extremely generous of them. God was just so good to us, sending us the things that we needed without us having to buy them. First, Peter erected the shuttering for the floor, mixed and poured the concrete himself and later built the walls. Nevertheless, for mixing the cement and carrying it up onto the roof, he decided some help would be required. It was an ideal opportunity to ask two other English friends to help out. Dave and Barry both had families and lived and worked on the island. They duly arrived at the crack of dawn to get the roof done in one day. Years later, Barry would end up in a wheel chair as the result of a stroke and have to move back to England. Dave would also have to return to England due to his wife's health problems and the difficulties of finding enough work to live. There are actually very few foreigners who have survived more than 10–20 years on Paros without having to give up and return to their own country. Often this was not by choice, but rather the result of adverse circumstances, usually health or financial reasons. We consider ourselves blessed to be one of the relatively few couples, who are still able to survive here all year around. There has been an influx of new Europeans over later years, but these are usually retired people with their own houses, so work, food and rent are not an issue.

The West Wing proved to be a great help to our ever-widening circle of activities. Some years later, we would decide that it would be rather good to have a second storage area. The first was full of beds, mattresses, and book shelves, yet I had an ever increasing number of old fashioned video cassettes, DVDs and yet more books. Printing the first one thousand copies of *To Greece and the Islands* meant having somewhere to keep them. It wasn't ideal, but it did allow me to have a supply available for people I talked to on the beach and around the island. We also still had our collection of two hundred plus, old LPs, which we were finding hard to throw in the bin, but the time needed to sell them on eBay seemed excessive and never seemed to materialise. Besides which, some of the real oldies we still enjoyed playing, even if we had had to throw out many others with unsuitable lyrics. Since I had been born again, I didn't want Santana singing "Black Magic Woman, You're gonna make a devil out of me"! Albums like that had been thrown away a long time before. However, a bit of Nat King Cole singing "L-O-V-E" is the sort of love and romance that married couples do well to enjoy from time to time. Once the second room was built, we finally had enough space to store everything.

Peter had already made us an outdoor shower because we often came back from the beach in summer covered in sand, and with a dog that loved rolling in the mud. Our neighbour's son had been showering outdoors for years and still continued to stand naked under the shower on his terrace long after we had arrived in the area. Fortunately, he was at such a distance so as not to render it indecent – well , at least not with my eyesight! Next, we thought we might as well have an outdoor toilet, so that when Peter was working in the garden he wouldn't have to tramp mud indoors to use the loo. It was just a toilet surrounded by a wall for privacy. It had no roof, but it was very handy. It also enclosed the shower, so we could shower without swimming trunks or bikini. Then, Peter decided to install a kitchen sink which someone was throwing out for their new kitchen to be fitted. This allowed me to clean the fish outdoors, as many Greek women do, and to easily change the water daily for twenty days while soaking the olives, before storing them in salt and vinegar. It also provided an area for cleaning paint brushes and other such messy jobs best kept out of the kitchen. Bearing in mind that many of these jobs are done wearing only a bikini or shorts and a T-shirt, you begin to get an idea of the completely different life-style we live here, compared to life in England or Belgium. Barbecues are just the normal way to grill all summer round, since it is much too hot to cook indoors and it does save dirtying the cooker. In the end, we also discovered that it was much cooler early morning in the West Wing, as it was on the shady, west side of the house, so we even slept out there sometimes in July and August, particularly if we had visitors in the house. It was all a bit basic and mosquito nets were essential as the place was infested in the summer. The problem resulted from the river bed one field across from us, a perfect breeding ground for the larvae. The open concrete water tank at the farm opposite didn't help matters either. As we walked past it each day on the way to the beach, we could see hundreds of wriggling little larvae worms swimming around. Fortunately, in latter years it was drained, painted white and the mosquito problem was reduced considerably.

The result of all this building was that many years later, in 2014, when the government introduced a scheme to register all changes made to the original plans of a house, we had to pay some 4,000 euros to draw up new plans. Still, it was well worth it, to have the extra space. Fortunately, by then, I had inherited some money and we could afford to pay that amount, as well as to build a nice, stone wall along the roadside of the land, making us all ship-shape and tidy. What with the 4,000 to pay and the cost of the wall at 3,000 euros, it was just as well my mum hadn't spent all her savings on cruises and new clothes before she died. She always did say that she wanted to leave something to help my sister and me out after she was gone, and she certainly did; God bless her! Some of the money she left us even enabled us to buy a new car, well, a nearly-new car. After selling the Land Rover, we had bought the little white Subaru mini bus, just as I had been guided to do at the Birmingham conference. It had seven seats and was just great for taking the kids on Sunday school outings to the Aqua Park. It was also practical for collecting broken-off branches and old pergolas for wood for the stove, as well as being ideal for taking the dog everywhere. When in latter years the gasket blew twice, after the second bill for 400 euros, there was nothing to do but to take it to the island scrap yard. As always, God provided for us magnificently when we went to find a new car. We wanted a Fiat Panda, a standard model with maybe 40,000 kilometres on the clock. The garage had nothing that old, but he did have a super Fiat Panda 4x4 with less than 5,000 kilometres on the clock. It was almost new, and it should have been way out of our price range. Amazingly, the salesman knocked 5,000 euros off the new price, as he had had it in the showroom for more than a year.

"It must be your lucky day!" he said, but we knew it was the favour of God and we were overwhelmed by His goodness. What a deal, what a miracle!

Just before the year 2000 ended, our German friends Klaus and Britta decided to marry. Klaus had been living on the island longer than most foreigners and Britta was the happiest of women since she had waited more than ten years for this event. They chose to use the town hall in the main town and this time my services weren't required to officiate, so I could relax. It is easy to see why so many foreigners want to marry in Greece. It was a December day, yet the weather was glorious, blue sky and sunshine. We gathered for the photographs on the terrace with the whole panorama of the bay of Parikia below us. What a group and what a mixture of nationalities we were. That is what life on Paros is all about. In England, I hardly knew anyone who wasn't English. Here we were Germans, English and Greeks together and we had all known each other for years. Klaus and Britta's friends, Frank and Irmo, had flown in from Germany and Theo, from the "Five F's restaurant", was the guest of honour. Klaus and Britta had been like part of his family for years and, in the early days, we had all spent many a happy day at his taverna on the beach at Mesada. Klaus had even helped him to build his house.

English Dave and Barry were there with their wives

and children. There would be no work mixing concrete that day. Giorgos from the Remezzo bar in Piso Livadi was there with his German wife, Utta. The hours we had all spent in the Remezzo bar in times gone by were innumerable. German Doris and Christina, both of whom had chosen a life on Paros were there, but would later return to Germany. In fact, fifteen years later, the group had diminished to only Klaus and Britta, Peter and I, Remezzo Giorgos and "Five F's" Theo. All the others had left. For those that have to earn a living, it is not as easy to live on a Greek island as many people would like to think.

The following year, in September 2001, things in my family were about to change. Mum and Dad decided to move from the elegant market town of Harrogate down to Albrighton to live closer to my sister. This was a source of comfort to me, knowing that they weren't quite so isolated as they had been in Harrogate. They were both approaching eighty and it seemed wise to be a bit closer to Margaret, without a two-hour drive in the car. It was also a good idea to settle where they would have her help if necessary in the future. They chose a small country village, Albrighton, near Shifnal, where my sister lives. It was also close to Cosford, where my dad had been stationed with the RAF during the Second World War. He was looking forward to seeing the old planes which they still flew on public open days.

They moved into another of what is called "sheltered accommodation" for the over-sixties, similar to the one where they had lived in Harrogate. These are blocks of privately-owned, self-contained, two-bedroomed apartments with communal lounges, fully maintained gardens and exterior decorating included. It is an ideal solution for elderly people who are still independent and yet may need some help. There was a warden on duty throughout the day and alarm-cords in each room if assistance was required, making it particularly safe for those who lived alone. For Mum and Dad, it was just a very nice flat in a very nice village exactly where they wanted to be. The communal lounge which, in theory, allowed people to chat and play cards or Scrabble with the neighbours was, in practice, only used for the once-weekly coffee morning and a few special events. I never saw anyone sitting there normally, as everyone preferred to watch TV in their own apartment.

I thought I'd let them settle in for a few weeks, enjoy their first Christmas in the new place, and then visit them in January. There was no apparent urgency, or so I thought. There was a Christian Conference in Croydon at the end of January. A Greek friend of mine was going, so I decided I would join her for three days and then travel up to see Mum and Dad. Little did I know that a silent clock was ticking and time was about to run out.

Having booked my flight in advance, with a return flight on 11 Feb, I then started getting messages from Margaret that Dad was not well. He had "water works" problems and they had taken him into hospital. During January he was in and out of hospital and finally scheduled for surgery the day after my conference ended. When I arrived at the hospital, I asked if I could stay with him day and night, Greek style. It was evident I needed to pray. I slept in a reclining chair at the side of his bed. He appeared to have caught an infection of the heart and the kidneys since he had entered hospital, and I just wanted to be close to him. It never occurred to me that he was about to die and go to glory. I was praying and expecting him to get well. Yet his breathing became laboured, he was put on oxygen, he ate less and less and, when I woke on the morning of 20 February, Dad's body was stiff and cold. He had gone. The doctors said he had had a pulmonary thrombosis. My mum was distraught and accused the hospital of killing her husband, since he had only gone in for a simple operation. I felt God had really let me down and, for weeks to come, my prayer time was distinctly lacking its previous intimacy. This was something God and

I were going to have to talk over and work through together. How could God have possibly let my dad die with all that prayer and left my mum to cope on her own?

The funeral was on my birthday, another birthday clouded with grief. Margaret had kindly asked if I wanted to make it a day later, but what difference did it make? I was hardly in the mood to celebrate my birthday, whatever day it was on. It was a miserable, cold, winter's day and I stood at the crematorium in borrowed black and navy clothing. I hadn't exactly packed for a funeral. The loss was terrible; for him it was an early promotion to glory, for us an aching emptiness. I knew I would see him again one day when I get to heaven, but I missed him now. How on earth was our mum going to manage without him?

8 SUDDEN DEATHS

The death of my dad caused much heart searching. I was suddenly acutely aware that my eighty year old mum was now living alone and the burden of her daily care fell to my sister, simply because I was more than a thousand miles away. Mum was already having memory problems and her whole personality seemed to be changing for the worse. We knew it was the onset of Alzheimer's, but we didn't realize it was going to get even worse. My life was firmly established here in Greece with absolutely no possibility of my going back to care for Mum. Even if I tried to bring her here to Greece to care for her, she would be totally isolated, unable to speak the language, with no access to an English speaking pensioners' club or English library, and there were few English speaking people of her age group. I felt it was unfair and impractical to even suggest that we isolate her in this way.

It was the death of British tourists and residents on Paros that really brought home the added complications of dealing with the deaths and funeral arrangements for non-Greeks on the island.

For as many years as I can remember, 10 June was an

annual reunion of the many foreigners who had holidayed on Paros year after year. It was the most perfect time of year for a get-together. Having spent the winter in the cold north of Europe, everyone was more than ready for the warmth of the Paros sun to soothe their weary bones and replace the deathly white pallor of winter with a deep tan. For these regulars, it was not enough to spend just two weeks hitting the beach at noon and roasting gently until the sun sank, causing the trees to cast shadows across the beach down to the water's edge as if to drink. No, three, or even four weeks, were required to deepen their initial light olive tan to an acceptably deep mahogany.

The wonderful thing about holidays here was that you could walk about the whole day clothed in very little: a bikini or shorts, maybe a light T-shirt, but most of the time even that was too hot to wear. Seven o'clock was about the earliest you could even think about a shower and wearing clothes, so many of the "regulars" would call at the local café, Gregory's, at the end of Logaras beach. Most of them had been coming to the Logaras side of Paros for five years or more, some as long as ten or twenty years. The real enthusiasts would make it twice a year, May-June and September-October. Gregory's was one of the few traditional cafés left on the island with round, blue, metal tables and blue, wooden chairs with hand-woven raffia seats. Most of the cafés on the island had replaced the traditional tables with some modern alternative in wood or white marble, and the chairs were director style canvas chairs in a variety of colours. The best thing about the place, apart from the magnificent view across the sea to Naxos Island, was Gregory and his son Manolis. Gregory's time-weathered face, his profusion of white hair and his sparkling blue eyes were a delight to behold. Manolis – rather tall for a Parian Greek – usually sat quietly in his chair in the corner of the terrace. He was always alert to the slightest change in the wind or current and ready to take his traditional, brightly painted fishing caique out for a catch. Gregory was never too busy serving to play a game of *tavli*/backgammon with his Greek friends, or even a foreigner wanting to learn. It was probably for this reason that, even after twenty years, all the wine, beer and soft drinks are still stored in fridges easily accessible to all: customers are expected to serve themselves, take an appropriate glass and even pull the cork of a bottle of wine. Of course, a real regular would probably drink *retsina*, the resinated Greek white wine which comes in half-litre bottles the same size, shape and cap as the beer, so no cork to pull. Payment is only made on departure and the whole business is run on the basis of trust.

So what was special about 10 June? It was Whistling John's birthday and, every year, he would arrive at Gregory's dressed for the grand event. With his multi-coloured checked suit, a selection of plastic whistles and his pre-recorded backing tracks, he would thrill us all as he trilled away, whistling the accompaniment to such classics as "In a Monastery Garden". When he dons his rubber monk's tonsured headpiece, the crowd suppresses their giggles, wondering whether to remain serious for the grand performance or to burst into gales of laughter. Muffled sniggers usually indicate that someone in the crowd is a newcomer and is not too sure what is *"de rigueur"* for such an occasion. John is not only quite the English gentleman and whistler, but also a talented artist: his charcoal portrait sketches are full of life and capture the subject perfectly. To this day, his portrait of Peter in all his glory with a full beard graces the wall in our dining room.

Amongst the gathering of spectators, there was no small number of musicians. They were mostly guitar players, such as Henk from Holland, Alain from Paris, English Becky living on Paros, "Banjo Bill" from Liverpool, Dave from Wigan and, last but not least, "Guitar Dave" who has lived in Marpissa for more years than I can remember.

In typical Greek style for a musical evening, it is usually

ten o'clock before the group arrive, settle down and begin to perform. To have a seat to sit on and a table for drinks requires an earlier start. The later arrivals have to settle for the steps or a stone pillar of the pergola as a leaning post.

Tuesday, 10 June 2003 was to be no ordinary night. John whistled, the musicians played and we sang our usual repertoire of 1960's to 1980's songs. Peter and I left the party in full swing around about midnight. We had long since stopped staying out until three in the morning, as in the early days. As we left to stroll the few minutes home along the back of the beach, we had no idea of the events that would occur that night.

The next day, we heard that Katherine, a regular English tourist at that time of the year, had decided to leave a little earlier than her husband, Alan. He had planned to just finish his beer, pay the bill and follow her back to their room in Piso Livadi. Since it was already late when she climbed into bed, Katherine had quickly fallen asleep. She was therefore rather surprised when she woke to find that Alan was not there beside her. Trying hard to rationalise the situation and not to fly into an immediate panic, she tried to convince herself that he was probably fine. He had most likely been persuaded to go back to the room of one of the guys for another drink and had fallen asleep there. After twenty-five years of marriage, she certainly wasn't worried that he had gone off with another woman.

As the day wore on, she walked back and forth between Logaras and Piso Livadi, asking everyone she knew if they had seen Alan, but all to no avail. As the sun was setting, she sat down in a local café with an English couple that lived on the island. On hearing of her dilemma, they promptly drove her to the local police station in Marpissa, just up the hill from Piso Livadi. Typically for such a small village, the office was closed for the evening and a call to the police station in the main town produced a predictable island response: "Well, it's too late to look for him now. Come over in the morning and make a full report".

They returned to Piso Livadi and joined other friends to discuss what they might do to find him. Kostas, a local builder that Peter had worked with, and his Swedish helper both volunteered to search the route along the cliff edge that Alan should have taken to return to his room. It was too dark to see anything at night and they hoped to find some clue the next day at first light. The road did pass high above the sea and there were places where it was a sheer drop down to the sea with no safety rail.

As promised, at sunrise the next day they searched along the cliffs. To their horror, there was Alan's crumpled body at the foot of the cliff, next to the sea. Tragically, the place at the bottom of the cliff where he fell was only 200 meters from the beach. It was so close that, had he been alive after the fall, he could have just swum or floated to the beach even if he was badly hurt. Either he was dead on impact, or he was unable to move. Perhaps he simply didn't think of it.

Understandably, Katherine was devastated. She was faced with all the complications of liaising with the local police, the British Embassy, and the funeral directors in the main town of Parikia who would store the body until it could be shipped back to England. Before that could occur, the body would have to be shipped to the hospital on Syros for a post mortem to determine the exact cause of death. It seemed a heart attack was the actual cause of death, but whether this occurred before or after the fall, we never found out.

It was at this point that an English lady living in Parikia arrived on the scene. Her name was Lornie and she lived all year round on Paros, running a second-hand bookshop. Her Greek was excellent, having been married to a Greek in England for some years. Finally, the Greek/English cultural divide and unfulfilled expectations caused the marriage break up. Lornie, ever willing to help someone in need, offered to translate between Katherine and the various officials. Since I was supporting and trying to comfort Katherine in all this, it was not surprising that Lornie and I made contact.

Somehow Lornie ended up reading my first book and, much to my astonishment, she phoned one day to say, "You got one!" This turned out to mean that she had said the prayer in chapter two to receive Christ as her Lord and Saviour. Lornie was born again! It may have been a tragic price to pay for her salvation, yet one would have to admit that it was a direct result of Alan's death that she found Christ. From that moment on, she became the most diligent attendee of our Sunday and Thursday meetings. To my recollection she rarely, if ever, missed a meeting in the next five years and she became a great help to me in the ministry in all sorts of practical ways. In fact, it was Lornie that painstakingly edited the original copy of my first book after the first print run! When she finally left the island years later, to return to England to care for her mother, it was a very sad loss indeed.

It was exactly a year later that I discovered the reason for Alan's tragic death at the young age of forty-seven years old. Whilst walking through Piso Livadi, I came across Katherine sitting with her mother, father and brother. They had come to support her on the first anniversary of Alan's death. She wanted to throw roses into the sea on Logaras at the spot where he had fallen to his death. I sat down to join them and we chatted at our table on the quay alongside the fishing boats. During the conversation, Katherine made a comment that was terribly tragic. She told me that Alan had ALWAYS SAID HE WOULD DIE AT forty-seven, that he would never make old bones. If only he had known that: "The tongue has the power of life and death" Proverbs 18:21, he would never have said such a thing. It was no one-off, idle comment, either. Over the years, he had repeatedly said it. Just as gravity is a physical law and a glass dropped from on high will fall to the ground and smash to pieces, so speaking death over oneself is a spiritual law which will bring death just as surely. It was fulfilled just as he had said. He died aged forty-seven!!

I took the opportunity to give each of them a small leaflet explaining how to become a Christian with a real relationship with Christ, not just a nominal church goer. After Alan's death, I wanted to be sure they had every opportunity to get right with Christ. It is often when people are hurting that they will reach out and take Christ's hand of help and comfort, when in the good times they consider they have no need of it.

In fact, I had had a telephone conversation with both Alan and Katherine in the February before Alan's death. One winter's night, they had phoned me from England. They had both read my first book and were very excited about it. Alan, in particular, told me how his father had just died and that he had just been made redundant. He was at an all-time low. After his father's death, while going through his belongings, he had found his father's Bible and had taken to reading it. I tried that night to encourage Alan, in particular, to make his decision to receive Christ, but he seemed unwilling at that stage.

I can only hope that, at some point between our conversation that night when he seemed so close, and before the moment of his death, Alan had remembered the words: "Everyone who calls on the name of the Lord will be saved". My hope is that, even if he had not received Christ before his fall, in those moments before his death he recognised his hopeless situation and cried out to Jesus, "Lord Jesus, save me!"

Alan was not to be the only friend we lost suddenly and because of his own careless words spoken in ignorance. Ashley died for exactly the same reason on the night of his 39th birthday. Ashley was an English man who had come to live on the island. In his early years here, like most people, he had found it difficult to earn a living. Although in England he had worked as a printer, on Paros he had had to turn to manual work, even heavy well-digging. Then, suddenly his fortunes changed. His father died and he inherited his father's home and capital. Suddenly, he could live in a comfortable, well-furnished, island apartment, having shipped much of the furniture over from England. Money was no longer a problem, so when his birthday arrived he threw a party at a local taverna, "Anna and Giorgos", the same place where we had celebrated Steven and Samantha's wedding. During the course of the evening, *three times* he came to me and SAID, "If I DIE TONIGHT I will die happy, I DON'T WANT TO LIVE TO BE FORTY, that's too old!"

"Ashley", I rebuked him, "don't say that, you don't understand the power of your words".

As usual, Peter and I left long before the party was over. The next day, we heard that, when the party had ended, he had insisted on riding his moped the short distance home in spite of the many drinks he had consumed. He had flatly refused the lifts offered to him by his friends. Short of punching him unconscious, there was no way to stop him since no one was able to hide his moped or keys. I felt such a failure that I had not put his words under the Blood of Jesus to render them powerless. I simply hadn't thought of it. In later years, it became something I do automatically whenever I hear negative words spoken. I had so much more to learn about the battle that goes on for every living soul.

Tragically, the list of those dying through spoken curses doesn't end there. Another friend was to die the same way. On the night of the Opening Ceremony of the Greek Olympic Games in 2004, a friend's son, Dimitris, crashed and died driving home from the fishing port of Naoussa, where he had been celebrating with his friends. He had offered a friend a lift to Aliki, just a few kilometres past his home, and had died on that extra leg of the journey home, the Aliki stretch of road. Like most of the Greek population that night, he was in high spirits and had decided to drive home rather than to take the safer option of a taxi. We heard that his friends had tried to persuade him not to drive, but he was young and carefree and had jokingly SAID, "WHY, WON'T YOU COME TO MY FUNERAL TOMORROW THEN?!"

The next day, a heavy cloud hung over their home as his mother and father wailed with grief, their eyes reddened after hours of weeping for their lost son. Little did they realise that those few careless words had probably cost Dimitris his life.

Another such incident was a family very close to us: in fact, the one that Peter had known the longest of all. They ran a taverna on the beach and were the people we had rented the house from in Marpissa. Peter had always stayed at their rooms and restaurant before living here. It was the summer of 2000 and the father had died suddenly having previously been in good health. We were confident he had gone to be with the Lord: he was one of those rare Greek men who truly loved the Lord and His Word. Each month, when we went to pay our monthly rent for their house in the village, we had had many good conversations about God with him and his wife. Before his death, we had shared the gospel with both of them, using the Greek calendar which we brought them every year in January. We also had read together a particularly good Christian tract with John 3:16 on one side and a prayer of repentance to receive Christ as Lord and Saviour on the other side. Each year, if we didn't arrive with the calendar in early January, he would ask if we could bring him one, he so enjoyed reading the daily Bible verses it contained. His faith in Christ was very evident and was expressed in his "good works": he took a young Albanian boy under his wing, caring for him and taking him everywhere with him on the farm. Many a time he would be seen on his diesel cart with the boy at his side. The cart would trundle along sounding "pap, pap, pap" at the grand speed of 10Km/hour. It was a small cart pulled by a rotavator; it was open to the air and had two bench seats up front, as well as space in the back for all the vegetables and tools. Unlike most people, he treated the boy almost as an adopted son, not just a worker.

He died a peaceful death at seventy-six, not sick in any way, as far as I was aware. Even so, his death was a great loss to all the family. His eldest son was inconsolable and many months later, I was told that he had SAID, "I DON'T WANT TO LIVE ANY MORE without my father. Within forty days his words had borne fruit and he too was dead at only fifty years old. What a tragedy. Yet again we realized the truth of the words: "The tongue has the power of life and death!"

In the same year that Alan had died and Katherine had suffered such mental torment over his death, Peter was undergoing his own trial by fire of a different sort. For years he had been regularly afflicted with excruciating pain in his kidneys. Long before coming to live in Greece, he had to have kidney stones removed by laser treatment in Belgium. Over the years, the high calcium content of the Paros tap water had done its damage, silently and stealthily converting the fine white marble of the Paros mountain water table into ugly grey stones accumulating in his kidneys. They would have looked quite at home on a lunar landscape or in the crater of the Santorini volcano. It was only years later, collecting information from a variety of sources, that we understood the dangers. The Greek *Spanakopita* (spinach pie) and the calcium in the Greek yoghurt and feta cheese were a perfect combination to feed the stone formation, even without the water calcium hazard. Spinach was something I rarely ate during my life in England, but here in Greece the list of delicious recipes for spinach is endless, *Spanakopita*, *Spanakorizo* (rice with tomato and spinach), and the delicious giant beans with spinach, feta and tomato sauce. Spinach, with a massive 750 mg per half a cup, is very high on the list of the oxalate content of common foods. Equally hazardous were cooked beetroot greens, another Greek delicacy where some people throw away the leaves in ignorance! Peanuts, chocolate and even his morning cup of tea had all contributed to the toll. For people without such a propensity to make kidney stones the way was open to enjoy such delights but, for the unlucky minority, great restraint is needed. Before we knew about these foods, going out to dinner in a restaurant had become an uncertain source of pleasure as, too many times, Peter would have to leave his food and return home to lie down until the pain had passed with the aid of suitable pain killers.

Many times we had prayed for the stones to be removed, expecting them to be dissolved, passed, or to just miraculously disappear. After prayer, Peter would sometimes be free from pain for a time, only to have our hopes dashed at a later re-occurrence. At other times, even with prayer, Peter had writhed in pain for between one and four hours!

Eventually, there was nothing to do but give in and take the hospital route again. This was not such an easy option with the life we were living in Greece, as I will explain. For more than ten years Peter had worked on the local building sites. Insurance stamps should have been given to him for each day worked but, at the end of a month's work (twenty-four working days), he would typically receive only eight to twelve stamps. At the time, this was the way that Greeks building houses would minimize the tax paid on the labour, thereby reducing the total building cost. It was, of course, illegal and, in theory, a worker could report the matter to the appropriate government office, but, in practice, he would then lose his job. Worse still, news of someone who had dared to do such a thing would fly around the whole community and he would be unlikely to ever find a day's work again. The good news was eight to twelve stamps a month would be enough to provide health cover for any hospital treatment and, at the time, we were oblivious to the loss of pension benefit this would cause in later years.

The complication was that, while Peter had a health insurance book until 2001, about that time he had been able to find fewer and fewer building jobs which would enable him to stay in the health insurance system. The boss and his son wanted to maximise their own stamps, so they avoided taking on extra workers wherever possible. More and more, Peter had been forced to take on small gardening jobs. The owners were only too glad to find someone reliable who would actually turn up and do the work, and the fact that he spoke Flemish, French, German, English and, now, Greek made communication much easier. With this work, we could eat and pay our bills but the downside was he had no health insurance.

The cost of each session of smashing the stones in his kidneys with lithotripsy was about 500 euros and he was likely to need anything from 4–6 sessions. It was a fortune to us and we just didn't have such an amount. Around this time, we heard that Greece does, in fact, have a welfare system for people who are genuinely unable to pay for hospital treatment. Thus began a long series of phone calls and correspondence with a Greek lady in an office in Syros. Peter had to produce electricity bills in our name to prove that we had been living in Greece for years, his expired health book, tax declarations and a whole list of other paperwork.

Maria in Syros became a beacon of hope to us that Peter would qualify for help and be able to go for treatment to end these years of pain and misery. Why prayer hadn't removed the stones, we had no idea, but, if prayer could identify a previously unknown system to cover his medical costs, Peter was just grateful to be able to take that route.

So, this was the background to how it came about that, early in January 2003, Peter took the ferry to Piraeus for a day of tests to determine what treatment would be required. On his return, the news was all bad. The stones were very large in both kidneys and they would probably have to perform keyhole surgery to remove them. They would begin with lithotripsy treatments to try to break the stones. We were about to discover the perils of life on a Greek island in winter, a reason why many Greeks and foreigners avoid island living.

Life was to become a series of night ships to Piraeus, leaving at 11p.m. on cold winter nights and arriving at 5a.m. in the morning. He then had to wait for the first trains to start running up to Athens and on to the Sismanoglio hospital. The cost of these monthly trips was an ever-mounting expense throughout the year and, when the wind raged eight Beaufort or more, Peter would have to spend a lonely night in a run-down hotel in a seedy part of the Piraeus port, so adding another thirty euros to the travelling cost. For someone that had earned the kind of money I had in England, this was all a very humbling experience. We were totally dependent on God to provide for us.

In between his trips he continued to earn a living with his gardening jobs, but, with his kidneys as they were, this was not always easy. One afternoon, Peter was in terrible pain after having worked in the cold wind all day. He struggled to eat the courgette soufflé that I had cooked for dinner, only to vomit the fruit of my labour before retreating to the bedroom. The best thing I could do was to go for a prayer walk on the beach. I just couldn't bear to watch him suffer so, writhing with pain. By the time I came home, the pain had subsided.

His return to hospital on 21 January produced yet more bad news. After injecting dye into his veins and taking X-rays of his kidneys, they discovered his left kidney was swollen to one and a half times its normal size. This meant that they couldn't operate until the swelling went down and, to get it to do that, they had to make a temporary bypass of the kidney, called a pig-tail. He would need this on both sides and would then have to wait another 2–3 months before they would be able to operate to remove the stones. In fact, it took much longer. Even for this first pig-tail operation there was no bed available, so that was another ferry trip back to Paros to wait. I was secretly relieved at the delay, still praying for a miracle. For the first time in weeks I felt that everything was going to be alright. We had a weekend of praise, expecting a miracle.

However, when a bed became available after a week of waiting, the stones were still there, in spite of all my prayers. Peter travelled up on the Sunday night to be admitted to hospital and I followed the next night to be with him for the operation on the Tuesday. Greek hospitals, then and now, require family members to provide day and night care for things that would be done by nurses in England and Belgium. So there we were, back in the hands of doctors, the expected miracle ever elusive. We would just have to accept that God had His reasons for sending us the hospital route.

They took Peter off to the operating theatre at 10a.m. I had just arrived at 7a.m. having travelled all night and was not feeling my best. The mental battle began; every thought of death bombarded my mind. I fought back speaking out Bible verses of life and healing. No wonder there was a book called *The Battlefield of the Mind*. I was so grateful when they brought him back to the room alive!

At 7p.m., a special Greek Christian friend, Joanna, arrived bearing gifts of food and books, but, more importantly, to pray with us. I felt such a deep love for her as we prayed together: what a wonderful thing it is to be a part of God's family! That night I slept peacefully under Peter's bed on my sleeping bag. The nurses turned a blind eye, knowing that we lived on an island. Peter was up and off early for X-rays and a urine test and, by lunchtime, we had been given the all-clear to leave the hospital. We just had to check through the hospital exit procedure and pay any amounts due. The operation was 600 euros, plus the cost of the bed at 88 euros a night for two nights, plus meals – so another 200 euros on top of the 600. I had prayed that we wouldn't have to pay for the operation and thankfully we were only asked to pay the 200 for the bed and meals. God is so faithful. None of the doctors had asked for the all too common *"fakelos"* (an envelope containing a cash gift for the doctor's pocket), for which we were most grateful. Whatever negative stories others may tell of Greek hospitals, we never had such experiences with God going before us.

The bus to the train station left from just outside the main hospital entrance and we didn't have to wait long for one to arrive. We jumped on, only to realise after five minutes that I had left my handbag on the seat at the bus stop. In my bag were our passports, money and house keys! What a disaster! We leapt off the bus, flagged down a taxi and asked for the hospital, only to discover we had found the only taxi driver who didn't know where the hospital was. He was just visiting the area and wasn't a local taxi. Finally, he worked out where the hospital was and we arrived at the entrance gates, only to find the bag was gone. Ever trusting that God had us in the palm of his hand and wouldn't fail us now, I asked at the little kiosk selling newspapers, drinks and chocolate, if he had seen a bag. Sure enough, he had it safe and sound – money, passport and keys intact. I could have jumped for joy. The man refused all offers of financial reward, so we gratefully left on the next bus, clutching my bag and Peter's suitcase.

Imagine our disappointment when we finally arrived at the port only to find that the ships were cancelled due to bad weather. After all we had been through we still couldn't go home; we had no choice but to book into a hotel and wait for the ship the next morning. Having refused the first offer of a room at 50 euros a night, we settled for a cheaper one at 35euros. By 7p.m. there was nothing to do but to go to bed so that Peter could rest on that cold, dark February night. By 9p.m. we were fast asleep in spite of the honking horns of the busy traffic down below.

We woke early at 6a.m. in the hope of the normal 7:30 ferry to Paros. Peter, ever keen or should I say, *desperate* to get home, leapt out of bed to go to the travel office for the latest news, "Sorry no, the ferry wouldn't leave until sometime between 10a.m. and noon". It was tempting to stay in bed and keep warm but, this being Greece, we understood that information is particularly subject to change. We decided to make a move for the ferry and board early, so ensuring it didn't leave early without us and to secure a seat for Peter. After four long hours waiting, it finally left and we then had another four and a half hours of the journey to suffer. Suffer was indeed the right word as two hours out to sea we sailed into a raging storm. My stomach felt awful, even with the excellent stabilizers of the new Blue Star ships.

It was a very grateful pair that finally disembarked into the bright Paros sunshine. The ordeal was over, for a while at least. Thank goodness we made it to the ship that day, as the next day there was a force nine Beaufort gale, it poured with rain and there was not a ship to be had!

That trip to Athens marked the beginning of a very long year of hospital visits during 2003. The stones that had taken years to accumulate in his body were not to be removed in a day, but a long series of monthly visits that would continue right through to February 2004. A final stubborn stone which survived the many sessions of lithotripsy would eventually be removed by keyhole surgery.

On Paros, the storms that had raged for three days were far from over. Within weeks, the worst floods in years hit Paros with a vengeance. The stone-built bridge in Naoussa harbour was completely swept into the sea, along with several cars, such was the fury of the swollen river as it coursed from the mountains down to the sea. Many houses were badly flooded and the furniture ruined in the basement rooms. Fortunately, our house is literally built on solid rock and suffered no damage at all. The land slopes gently down to the sea, so even a heavy deluge of rain runs from the top north-east corner to the south corner, two metres high above the ground. We had never planned it to be so high above the ground and the reason is in itself quite a "Greek" story.

We had originally estimated about two million drachmas, (£6,000), for the foundations and concrete frame for the house. This included one day's work to dig the foundations with two bulldozers: one with the hammer to break the rock and the other with the shovel to move the rock away. Three days later, they were still digging at the south end of the house where the *sterna*, our water tank, was to sit under the terraces. When Peter returned home on day three, he was horrified to see this enormous hole in the ground which was certainly big enough for a modest-sized swimming pool!

"Stop, stop!" he cried, "what's going on?"

"We're digging the water tank. You can't have too much water you know!"

"It's not the water we don't want, it's the cost of the concrete to build the tank to store it in that's the problem." Our estimated concrete cost had just doubled overnight.

What we didn't realise was that when it did rain heavily we would be high above the flood. We avoided the many problems others had created by building illegal basements under the planned ground floor accommodation. The Paros floods that year left a trail of soggy, wet mattresses and ruined furniture. It was yet another illustration of "A man makes his plans, but the Lord determines his steps."

The man was also right in saying, "You can never have too much water". Since we moved into the house in 1994, the price of water has rocketed, yet we have a free supply of pure rain water from the roof. For years we only used it to water the lower vegetable garden, tomatoes, peppers and fruit trees, but later on we realised the potential to utilise it in the house.

A visiting English Christian family gave us a very generous gift of £500. For a long time we had been aware that the summer droughts were getting longer and the winter of 2006–2007 had brought almost no rain at all. It was questionable if we would make it through the summer season without long periods of water restrictions and supplies cut off by the Paros Water board, DEYAP. After much prayer, we felt that it would be in order for us to use this gift to buy a water pump. This would then pump the water from the water tank into the house for use in showers, toilets and especially for the washing machine. Time and time again in the summer, the supply was so slow that a mere dribble was all the washing machine had available; a normal one-hour program seemed to take an eternity to complete. Once the pump was installed, we had a steady flow of water to wash clothes, shower and generally get on with life oblivious to the water shortages suffered in the houses and rooms around us. The Lord certainly had provided for our needs through His people.

We also realised that, if the winter rainfall wasn't sufficient to fill all seventy cubic metres of the water tank from the rain on our roof, our neighbour Tassos had a well, perfectly situated next to our land. He was more than happy for us to pump water from his well into our tank during January and February while it was raining, and his water supply in the well would rapidly replenish. An apparent catastrophe at the time of excavation had turned into a real source of blessing!

9 GREEK OLYMPIC GAMES

In 2004 the Olympic Games returned to Greece. While everyone else had their eyes on the athletic and other Olympic events, we had quite a different focus: Operation Gideon! Hellenic Ministries, a Greek Missionary Group based in Athens, were targeting the Cyclades Islands, where we lived, for a major Gospel outreach. With their yacht, the *Morning Star*, and teams made up of Christians from around the world, there would be a major distribution of New Testaments on the islands, plus three days of preaching the gospel on the streets. We were to deliver by hand 950 Modern Greek New Testaments to homes on Paros and Antiparos. Paros was allocated a team from America – Holly, Terry and Julie, plus Martha, another Christian from Australia. The Hellenic Ministries group were very special people to me as the founder of the group, Costas Macris, was the man whose story God had used to direct me to Greece way back in 1985. He was one of the three men sentenced to three and a half years in prison for giving a New Testament to a young Greek boy under the age of eighteen. His sons now headed up Hellenic Ministries.

I was thrilled that, not only had Paros been included in the outreach to the Cyclades Islands, but the yacht *Morning Star* would come to our island in August. It would be captained by Alex Macris, one of Costas' sons. Finally, we would have some help to preach the gospel on the island after fifteen years of trying to do it without much support. The outreach would last nine days. Initially, there would be three days of prayer, fasting and prayer walks. The second three-day block would include evening gospel presentations on the streets while people were strolling around after the heat of the day. Then, in the final three days, we would distribute 950 Greek New Testaments around Paros and the adjacent island of Antiparos.

On the morning of the first day of prayer and fasting, we all met in the main town of Parikia and began to walk around the perimeter. This was a strategy based on the story of Joshua, who had marched around the city of Jericho for seven days, praising God and praying for victory. God had told them that on the seventh day the city walls would fall down. Parikia had no physical walls to fall down, but it did have strong spiritual walls that needed to fall in order to usher in a wave of the Holy Spirit. Then the people would be free to move from empty religious rituals into a genuine relationship with the Lord God himself. We walked the streets in the blistering heat, pasted with high factor suntan lotion and wearing hats to protect us from the relentless heat of the August sun. For those of us who lived on the island and were somewhat acclimatised to the heat, it was a challenge both physically and spiritually. For the American visitors, used to much cooler climates, they needed an extra supply of determination to keep going.

On the second day, we were led to travel up to the radio masts above Lefkes village, the highest point on the island. Many times in the Bible, God's people went up on mountains to pray. We took with us a wooden stake on which we had written a verse from the Bible, 1 Timothy

2:5: "For there is one God and one mediator between God and men, the man Christ Jesus". In doing this we felt that we were declaring into the heavenly realms the Lordship of Christ, giving Jesus Christ the honour that is due to Him and Him alone. This is particularly important in a country where many people use Mary, the mother of Christ, as an intermediary to pray to God. Later, we walked around Naoussa and the small village of Kostos in the mountains praying for the people there.

On day three, we targeted the villages of Marpissa, Logaras, Piso Livadi, Marmara, Prodromos and Drios, praying as we walked; these were the villages in the area closest to our home base of Logaras.

The island was then ready for the preaching. The *Morning Star* was moored in the picturesque harbour of Naoussa, a thriving tourist centre in the summer months. We met on the yacht during the morning to learn some songs together and communicate the strategy for the evening's evangelism. At nine in the evening we met at the bridge in Naoussa and sang some Christian choruses. Then, a young man from America preached a classic gospel message, which was translated into Greek enabling Greeks and English speaking foreigners to understand at the same time. Many of the Greeks passed by without even listening. Instead of being excited that we were fellow Christians reaching out to a world of lost, lonely and hurting unbelievers, to them (since we were not Greek Orthodox Christians) we were classed as heretics, false teachers and mistakenly labelled us as Jehovah's Witnesses. At the end of the gospel message, members of the team circulated amongst those who had gathered to listen and some fruitful conversations ensued. We had made a start.

That night sleep eluded me, tired as I was after the fourth day of the program. The gospel had been preached, but in a way that only told what every Greek had heard year after year. The message of Jesus Christ crucified to be the perfect sinless sacrifice for our sins, to bring us forgiveness, raised from the dead that we might have eternal life with Christ and His Father God, if we believe this.

What they didn't know and hadn't been told was that it is by faith alone in what Christ did that they would receive forgiveness and eternal life. It was not dependent upon a lifetime of good works, helping the poor, visiting the sick and, maybe, if they were good enough and did enough, they would finally go to heaven. Tragically, they were still trying to pray people into heaven at their funeral and forever after at memorial services.

It had not been explained to them that there is a difference between empty religious tradition and having a living relationship with Jesus Christ by being spiritually reborn at some point in their life. Most of the Greeks I had talked to thought they were born again as babies at baptism, even though babies are totally unable to believe. When I asked if they thought they would go to heaven the reply was usually, "Well, it depends if I have been good enough."

As I lay in bed, a whole gospel message streamed into my mind, rather like downloading a file from the Internet. By the time I awoke, all I had to do was write it down. I have not had such an experience either before or since. The words burned within my very soul. I just had to find Alex Macris to tell him what had happened and to ask him if I could share the message the next day in Lefkes. Much to my relief he agreed in spite of me being a woman which, in some churches, can pose a bit of a problem. We arranged to meet in the square in Lefkes the next evening.

On arrival there were plenty of people milling around. It was the peak holiday week of the year. Thousands of Greeks had come over to Paros from Athens for their annual summer holiday and to return to their island roots. The main festival on 15 August to celebrate the purported Ascension to heaven of Mary was now over. The more devout Orthodox Christians had ended their forty day partial fast of no meat, restricted consumption of oil, dairy and so on. Now, they were free to eat as they wanted and the nearby restaurant balcony was packed. They would hear every word. Groups of people of all ages were sitting on the low walls around the square, the benches were full and children played under the tall eucalyptus trees. This was the village where I had lived and prayed during my first month on Paros in 1989, fifteen years earlier.

As we launched into the first song, "Lord I Lift Your Name on High", followed by "My Jesus, my Saviour", my heart soared. This was what it was all about; this was why I had come to Greece. Finally, we had the support we needed to preach the gospel to the Greeks on Paros; we were a group of about twenty. Alex Macris would translate into Greek as I spoke in English. Again Greeks and foreigner tourists would hear the message. And so I began to speak:

"I first arrived on Paros in 1989 and I lived in Lefkes for the month of April. My name is Barbara, I'm English, and I have lived on Paros for fourteen years. I love Greece and especially the Greek people. You are so warm, so friendly and so kind in opening your homes to strangers and offering such wonderful hospitality. It is because I care for you so much that today I want to talk to you about your eternal destiny.

The New Testament tells us: "If anyone is in Christ he is a new creation, the old has gone and the new has come". Today, I want you to ask yourself if the new has come into your life, if can you remember a day when you became a new person? Can you remember a day when you no longer wanted just the passing pleasures of life and became interested in the things of God, in Jesus and in the Bible; a day when your old, bad habits no longer seemed so attractive; a day when you felt an inner peace?

It didn't happen when you were baptised as a baby, you didn't have an old life then for the old to go. For me, it happened when I was thirty-three years old, when I asked

Jesus to be my Lord and Saviour. I then genuinely repented of my sins, of which there were many. Overnight I changed. I suddenly wanted to read the Bible and find out as much about God and Jesus as possible. People that I worked with in the office in London could see the change in me. If you think about it, you'd expect to see a change in someone if the Holy Spirit of Almighty God came to live in them.

The Gospel of John tells us: "No one can see the kingdom of God unless he is born again", which means born a second time, born of the Holy Spirit. "To all who received him, believed in his name, he gave the right to become children of God" We have to receive Him to inherit eternal life. Have you done that?

You see, it is by receiving Jesus, believing that He is the Son of God, that we inherit eternal life. Just being a good person, doing good things and helping people is not enough. These are what the Bible calls "works", but no one can ever be good enough. That's why God says, "For it is by grace you have been saved through faith and this not from yourselves, it is the gift of God – not by works, so that no one can boast" It's not "See what a good person I am and all the good things I do".

Let me help you to understand. Suppose I sweep the streets of Lefkes everyday for a month. It is a good thing to do, the people of the village are pleased and I am helping people.

Let's suppose at the end of the month I go to the *Koinotita*, the town council, and I ask for my wages. They won't pay me because I never signed a contract with them for me to do the work in the first place. First, I must have a legal agreement to do the work and sign the contract, then with that, I can do the work.

Spiritually, first I must sign the contract with God; I enter into a covenant relationship with Him. I need to be spiritually born, by repenting and receiving forgiveness in Jesus' name.

Second, I must do the work to receive my reward, but not to receive my salvation. Salvation is by faith alone in what Jesus did at the cross, not by what I have done. My good works will determine my reward when I get to heaven, but will not determine whether I get to heaven!!

I find it so sad that when I ask Greek friends if they think they will go to heaven when they die, many say, "Well, it depends if I have been good enough". What is the point of having a Saviour Jesus, if you don't believe He will save you?

No one knew that *the Samina* would sink that night in 2000. No one knows if they will have an accident and die early. No one knows when Jesus will return and take the believers to heaven. Will you be ready if it happens to you? Are you a new creation in Christ Jesus? Have you been born again of the Spirit? Do you believe in His name, Jesus, which means Saviour?"

At this point we handed out small tracts/leaflets containing a simple prayer for people to declare their faith in Jesus as the Son of God, to receive Him as their Lord and Saviour and to receive forgiveness for their sins.

For the first time in all my years in Greece, people began to take the tracts and read them instead of throwing them to the ground, as had happened on previous occasions. Some people even came and asked for one.

As I lay in bed that night, I felt that wonderful sense of fulfilment that comes with the knowing that I had done what God had told me to do. The commission of Jesus to all believers is to: "Go and make disciples of all nations" Matthew 28:19. It was really something special to hear Him tell me a specific message to preach.

After the whole outreach was completed, only one person on the whole of Paros actually contacted Hellenic Ministries and asked for a free New Testament. That person was a lady from Lefkes! I never did meet her; she wished to remain anonymous and asked for the New Testament to be delivered to the bakery. I gladly took it there, just thrilled that someone had heard and responded to the message God had given to me.

We had chosen three towns to preach in for the three consecutive evenings. The final night of the outreach was in Parikia, the main port. That night I was asked to share briefly my testimony of becoming a Christian and how it had changed my life, but not to preach as I had in Lefkes, in order to give a young man the opportunity. Somehow, my simple testimony didn't have the same anointing as the night before, I felt awkward and it didn't flow. The gospel was then preached, but again, as on the first night, no mention was made of salvation by faith, not by works. For the Greeks and many others I really believe this is the key to their salvation. They have always believed that getting to heaven depends upon what they do rather than what Christ did.

Now the three days preaching were over it was time to deliver the New Testaments – all 950 of them!! Teams of volunteers had spent days in Athens filling specially printed love bags with a New Testament signed by the Orthodox Church bishops, together with colourful, appropriate tracts and a gospel newspaper. We left them on doors and gate handles, in fact everywhere we could see that people were living. Thank goodness we had the girls from America and Australian Martha to help. It took us just over the three days, and Martha and I spent the fourth morning delivering the last bags around Logaras until she left at two o'clock. I wanted to be sure all our neighbours got one! Fortunately, an extra team of girls that were originally on Ios came to Paros to help us – Beth, Nicole and Laura. By the time we had finished, there was such a feeling of satisfaction in a job well done. New friends had been made and, years later, Holly from Hawaii and Martha from Australia would return to Paros to visit us.

10 BAPTISMS

As the years passed, one of the things that never ceased to amaze me was the number of baptisms we were asked to conduct for people of all ages and many nationalities. So many people had only been baptised as infants when they were not capable of believing in Jesus as the Son of God or confessing Jesus as Lord. As far as my understanding goes, the idea that a third party godparent can do the believing for you is totally non-scriptural and appears not once in the New Testament. Since I had been baptised as an infant, or "christened" as it was called in the Presbyterian Church, I was very sympathetic to people who had ended up in this situation. I had chosen to be baptised at the age of thirty-three, some two months after receiving Christ. The delay was due to the fact that it took me about that long to start going to church and for the first baptism ceremony to take place.

Even more amazing to me than the number of people we baptised was how some of the people found us or came to be with us at all. One such example was an elderly South African couple. It was the morning of a sizzling hot summer's day and I was at home when the phone rang. It was Lornie from the second hand bookshop in the main town; she had someone in the shop who wanted to talk me. The couple introduced themselves and said that they had read my book and would like to meet up with me. I'm not in the habit of jumping in the car to go into town at every request, but I felt that this was something I should do. In spite of the heat I jumped into the car, drove the 15km into Parikia and met them for a coffee.

They were Christians and regularly attended church in their home town in South Africa. Reading the first edition of my book, which included several stories of people being baptised, they had felt that they too should be baptised as adults since they had only ever been baptised as babies. I was delighted to hear that the Holy Spirit had used my book to speak to them so clearly.

"That's wonderful", I said, "You will be able to do that at your home church when you return to South Africa."

"Well, that's the problem," they replied. "At our church they only baptise infants, so it wouldn't be possible for us. We were rather hoping you might be able to baptise us here on Paros."

I was somewhat taken aback but, if that was what they felt they should do, who was I to deprive them of their baptism? I'm sure Philip wouldn't have said to the Ethiopian Eunuch, "Actually, no, I have to check with the elders first."

"Yes, if that's what you really want, but usually my husband and I together baptise people. When are you leaving the island?"

"Tomorrow!" they replied, which didn't give us much time at all.

"Alright, I suppose I could walk fully dressed into the water here and baptise you myself, but it would be much better if, maybe this afternoon, you could come over to our side of the island, then both Peter and I could baptise you. First, I would like to read some scriptures to you, including some from Romans 6."

So, it was agreed that they would take the 2p.m. bus over to us. They would arrive at 3p.m., we'd baptise them, and they could return with the 5p.m. bus to pack and be ready to leave the next morning. And that was what happened! We met them at the bus stop, then sat under the big tamarisk tree at the far end of Logaras beach and read several scriptures including Romans 6:3–7: "We were therefore buried with him through baptism into death, in order that just as Christ was raised from the dead through the glory of the Father, we too may live a new life".

Each of them repeated after me a prayer of repentance to affirm their faith in Jesus Christ as Lord and Saviour, and then Peter and I baptised them in the name of the Father, the Son, Jesus Christ and the Holy Spirit, making sure they went completely underwater before helping them to resurface. I felt rather humbled to think that God would choose to use us to baptise people who had been believers much longer than we had. Although we never heard from them again, we did receive a lovely letter from a neighbour of theirs. They had lent my book to her and told her about their baptisms. It was all most encouraging.

It wasn't only older Christians that requested baptism. One winter, at the end of November, we decided to go to a choral evening at the Catholic church in the main town. A group of young Americans were among those singing and, as we were chatting to them at the end of the recital, it came up in the conversation that we had a house church meeting on Sunday mornings. The whole group decided to come over the next Sunday and so it was that young Stephen, about twenty years old, and five of his friends from the Art School came to join us. I have no recollection what I taught on that day but, at the end of the meeting, Stephen approached me and said that he felt the Holy Spirit wanted him to be baptised. As per my usual response, I told him how marvellous it would be to be baptised when he returned to his home church in America.

"No," he replied, "I want to do it now."

"Won't your parents be rather disappointed not to be present?" I asked him.

"No, I think they will be very pleased" was his reply. So off again into the rather chilly sea of late November for another baptism!

Another surprising request came from an elderly man with a youth ministry, who had been in the church most of his life. He came to join us one Sunday morning with Annamarie, our Swiss friend. He was also Swiss and had come to visit her for a week or so. His visit was at the same time that my niece was staying with us and she usually sacrificed some prime sunbathing time on a Sunday morning to join us for our worship meeting and to take Communion. For years, I had been trying to encourage her to be baptised; she knew that both her mum and I had been baptised as adults even though we were both christened as babies as she had been. On this particular morning, I had felt to use a teaching on water baptism from a Christian TV station. James Merritt gave a clear teaching on baptism, pointing out that there were no infant baptisms in the New Testament. It is unlikely that either the Roman centurion's family or the Philippine jailer had babies living with them. These two stories from the book of Acts are often used to try to justify infant baptisms. I had hoped that such a clear and simple message would speak to my niece's heart and she would finally ask to be baptised.

Imagine my complete surprise when I asked who would like to be baptised and this Swiss man was the one who responded! He felt that the Holy Spirit had been dealing with him for quite some time about being baptised. He did not want to delay until his return to Switzerland as he felt that it would be rather embarrassing to be baptised there after so many years in ministry. So that was it, swimming costumes on and down to the beach for a baptism. My disappointment at my niece's silence on the subject was partially overcome by my joy at the Swiss gentleman's request.

Sometimes, it was people living on Paros that requested baptism. It was one such local request which turned into a double baptism. It occurred a few years after my trip to Colorado when Amy and Robin hadn't been able to come to Greece due to the anti-American sentiment. Finally, Greek emotions towards America had calmed down and it was possible for them to travel safely to Greece. They arrived on Paros with some friends from their church, Calvary Chapel. Chris was the youth pastor and Di, his wife, came too. For some years, I had been having coffee with a lady who became a special friend and we had often talked about Jesus. She was a Catholic and so, like many others, had only been baptised as an infant.

Much to my delight, in the summer of 2002, she decided to be baptised as an adult. Her mother was also visiting and she too wanted to be baptised. What a joy it was to go to a small, nearby, sheltered cove, to sit on the beach with our Bibles reading the scriptures on baptism, and then to baptise them. Peter was working, so couldn't join us for this happy event. With Chris on one side and me on the other, we baptised first the one and then the other. I still have the printed photos, the last before the era of digital cameras and downloads to "My Pictures" took over. Many years later, in 2014, I dug out the old photos and took them down to their house for a visit with her mother and her brother, who also lives on the island. It brought back happy memories of a wonderful day. I wanted to plant the seed in her brother's mind that he needed to be baptised, too.

Of course, it was always disappointing when we baptised people who lived on the island if they didn't then continue to worship and to join us in fellowship on Sundays. No doubt this often happens in many larger churches but in a smaller group it is rather more noticeable. Conversely, it was wonderful when we baptised people into the body of Christ and they did continue to join us most Sundays. It always felt like a family gathering when we met in our house, something perhaps larger groups in formal church buildings don't experience in quite the same way.

Years ago, Eli, a Bulgarian lady, had come to live on Paros. After working many years on the island, she had married a local Greek man that we knew. She was such a lovely lady, slim and attractive, with beautiful long, auburn hair cascading over her shoulders. As well as being an excellent cook of all the traditional Greek dishes and sweets, she kept the house spotless. Her husband had indeed found a Proverbs 31 wife of noble character. Eli and I became friends over a number of years. She helped me with my Greek and I helped her with her English. We went for walks together and drank coffee some afternoons at her house, often exchanging recipes for the lovely biscuits or a cake that she had made for my visit. In all this, of course, we spoke many times about the Lord and read passages from the Bible together. Her brother in Bulgaria had been born again and a house group met in his home; I expect that he was praying for her salvation, as I was. Twice, Eli had serious health issues and came to me in much distress – once with meningitis, a very serious disease – and she wasn't getting better, but worse. Both times we had prayed together; it had proved to be a turning point in the illness with healing following. She knew it was the answer to our prayers and we gave Jesus all the glory. Regrettably, for years, it was difficult for her to join us on Sunday mornings as her husband would want her to join him with this job or that around the home and the garden. The Greek culture is very different to the Northern European culture where a married woman is free to spend at least some of her time as she chooses. The contrast with the freedom I experienced in my own married life was quite noticeable.

It was at some time of difficulty that Eli realised that, without the strengthening of the Holy Spirit that she received when she joined in our meetings, she just couldn't face the challenges of everyday life. Yes, she was reading her Bible and yes, she was praying, but all alone, so she had little teaching. From that point on, she decided to take a stand and join us weekly. She hung on every word, took notes and gradually she began to blossom like a beautiful rose. It was not long before she asked to be baptised, and what a lovely group we made that summer's day in May as we walked down to the beach together for her baptism. There was Swiss Annamarie, Jenny from New Zealand, Albanian Dorina and her little daughter Resmina, as well as Peter and I. After the baptism in water, we laid hands on her to receive the gift of the Holy Spirit.

Eli's husband, like many Greeks baptised as infants into the Greek Orthodox Church, never really understood why she needed to come to us for Bible study and teaching. Why wasn't it enough just to go to the Orthodox church, light a candle, kiss the icons, make a sign of the cross, then leave as everyone else did? Nevertheless, with the passage of time, he could see the change in her, the lightening of her spirits and the peace that she now had in her heart. He even started to read the Greek New Testament, in modern *"Dimotiki"* Greek for himself.

We have since baptised many others who have come to our Logaras church. There were some who had never been baptised at all, having been brought up in non-Christian homes. When they finally reached the point of receiving Christ, we would always teach them the purpose of baptism and follow through with actual baptism if they were willing. Some of these people have moved away and are settled into churches in Greece or other countries.

11 DAILY LIFE

Our life on Paros became an interesting mixture of the ordinary everyday things of life intertwined with all the spiritual events going on at the same time. Even the everyday events were a strange mix of so many good things of a Greek lifestyle, together with other customs which were so very English.

Every spring, preceding the Easter celebrations, there was a flurry of activity which included freshly painting every wall white to cover the trail of rain tracks which had trickled down exterior walls from fences, pergolas and drain pipes. The green moss, which had crept across terraces during the winter, was carefully scraped off and beautiful Parian stone terraces were restored to their original glory. The garden, which had been wrapped in a shroud of clover throughout the winter months, needed to be stripped of the lush green covering to reveal the flowers and young plants hiding beneath their warm, winter blanket. All of this activity had to be slotted in between the usual tasks of life: cooking, washing clothes and cleaning the house. My cooking now involved tasks such as cleaning and gutting fish, (something I never did in

England), then sun-drying them sprinkled with oregano ready to barbecue. There was more than enough work to fill anyone's day for several weeks in March and April before the summer season when all the visitors would arrive.

For me, this was far from all I was trying to do on a typical day in March. As well as each week preparing a Bible teaching for Sunday, plus spending time with the many lost souls I met, things had a nasty habit of cropping up unexpectedly. Sometimes, people were so much in need of help that everything else just had to go on hold, even the painting.

One such example was my friend Doris. She had been looking after someone's horse when she was trapped between the horse and the fence and broke her hip. We got a phone call to say that she was in an Athens hospital and needed someone to go and help her with all her paperwork to get her out and help her to get home. None of her other German friends seemed able to go and help her, so it fell to me to catch the night ferry up to Piraeus, then get a taxi which would arrive at the hospital around midnight. I had to find my way to her through the maze of corridors and then get her ready to leave by 11a.m. the next day. Since she couldn't walk, and she needed to keep her leg horizontal, she was going to need an ambulance. Looking back, it was amazing that I ever managed to do all this, what with the language to overcome and the mountain of hospital paperwork to wade through. It was only with the help of God that we finally got her settled onto the ferry for the five-hour journey to Paros. Getting her from the lower car deck up to the cabins was challenging but, with the help of the ferry staff, we made it on and then off again at Paros. Another ambulance was waiting at the port and we brought her to our house to stay until she was well again. Her house may have been in a very picturesque location, but the road to it was only really suitable for donkeys, tractors and Land Rovers. It was entirely unsuitable for an ambulance to negotiate. We expected that she would stay with us for about a month.

The next morning, I was rather surprised to find Doris in some distress. She had pain in her chest, difficulty breathing and a fever. What was this all about with just a broken hip? I called Lornie, who had been a nurse in England. From the description of the symptoms, she immediately spotted the probability of an embolism from her leg to her lungs. I was to call an ambulance immediately. After an overnight stay in the main town hospital, X-rays showed an embolism on her lungs and she would have to go back up to Athens on the ferry. Oh dear, not again! So began another week-long stay in hospital with me sleeping on the floor or a chair by her bed. She needed me there to help her with the bed pan, amongst other things, but during the week we also had many hours to spend just chatting to pass the time, which provided me with the ideal opportunity to talk to her about receiving Jesus as her Saviour. Exhausted by days with no proper sleep, it was a great relief when help finally arrived from one of her German Paros friends. At last I could go home and sleep in a bed!

Some days later, Doris eventually realised that she would have to go back to Germany, a prospect that she wasn't looking forward to at all. Her friends at the hospital finally persuaded her that it would be for the best and made the necessary arrangements. Doris never did come back to live permanently on Paros. She returned briefly, some months later, just to retrieve some of her belongings and to let go of her rented house. It was the end of an era in her lifetime.

After a few weeks respite, the next needy soul was demanding attention. Our Swedish friend broke his arm in a motor bike accident and he needed help. Fortunately, this time Lornie would go to Athens to help him instead of me. We might just get the painting finished before the visitors arrived for the summer and even have time to enjoy the luxury of picking *karfa*, the wild asparagus which grows in the mountains ready for collecting in late April or early May.

We somehow still managed our weekly Sunday meetings and we were really blessed to have two Filipino power station workers with us. Wencee was the leader of a team of about ten workers who had a contract to install a new turbine at the Paros power station in Naoussa. This was not a quick job and would require them to stay on the island for several months.

We'd actually visited the power station a year or so before at the invitation of a Polish man working there that we had met. One of Wencee's team, Nathan, also wanted to join us, so, if there were no technical problems, they were free to travel over most Sundays. While Wencee came from a large city, it was particularly interesting to hear Nathan's stories about life in the small villages out in the islands. We learnt that pastors of the churches often did not have much money for daily necessities and many were without shoes. It seemed that 100 euros was enough to buy shoes for many pastors out there, and Nathan would be able to distribute a gift that we wanted to send expressly to buy shoes. It really was amazing: all the nationalities we came into contact with. Later in the year, we would lose Wencee and Nathan to another Greek island, Xios, where they would work on the power station. They spent many months away from home separated from their families, but the wages in Greece were definitely worth it for a time.

In earlier years, groups of Kenyan ladies, who cleaned rooms near Naoussa, had visited us. Later we enjoyed the decade of the Nigerian visitors: Evi, Happy, Raph and Victor. Sometimes, they would have problems with their employers who would hold back their wages, so we would have to pray in their wages. Many were sending almost all the money earned back to Nigeria to support other family members. It was a hard life for them and they welcomed their weekly time of refreshing at our well of living water in a dry and weary land. We would pray for their family members to be healed, baptise any who were not baptised as adults, and generally try to be as supportive as possible.

Evi was engaged to be married to a man in Nigeria who had been selected by her family. She had not even met him. The possibility of such a situation is completely alien to our Western European minds. At one point, she left to fly to Nigeria complete with her Greek-made wedding dress and several other outfits dug out from our wardrobes. I had never been quite able to throw away a lemon chiffon evening dress I had, even though it no longer fastened. Like most women, I was sure that someday I would lose weight and wear it again. That day never came as my waist thickened with advancing years, so the opportunity to bless a slim, young woman about to marry seemed the perfect time to release it. Imagine our surprise when she returned unmarried! She had decided she just couldn't marry the man, even if her family had chosen him. Years later, she left Paros, returned to Athens and married a young man she met at the Nigerian church there. All was still not to go well.

Her husband longed to be a pastor and, for some reason, they wanted to go to Canada. He wanted to go to Bible College there. Work was difficult to find in Athens and, after long waits for Greek bureaucracy to grind into action, Evi finally received the papers she needed to travel to Canada, or so she thought. The plan was that she would go on ahead; she would find work looking after children for a family and then her husband would follow on. Her flight was via Switzerland. Imagine our surprise when we heard that she was remanded in custody in Switzerland and not allowed to travel on to Canada because the papers she had been given and paid for were not correct. In addition, she was pregnant with their first child and gave birth to her daughter in an area for illegal immigrants in Switzerland. Years later, as far as we know from Facebook, she is still there, separated from her husband and her dream of going to Canada. This is not an isolated incident, and when you come into contact with as many Africans, Albanians and other immigrants as we do, it becomes clear that immigrants outside the European Union suffer many injustices while living here.

An Albanian man we know has spent more than 3,000 euros, trying to get Greek IKA employment insurance which he was entitled to. After paying solicitors to help for three years, he had still not obtained his papers. It keeps the solicitors in business at the expense of poor immigrants, who then get behind with their rent. The absence of insurance deprives them of their government winter assistance payments as seasonal workers, as well as child allowance and other benefits. Finally, after putting the problem on the prayer chain for many months, it was approved. The typical European pensioner who comes to live here, but doesn't need to work here, is usually totally unaware of the injustices going on in the lives of those less fortunate around them. Attending various musical and arts events that Paros is famous for in the summer months, they live a life separated from the hardships of families around them. It's not that these situations don't exist in many countries, but on a small island where everyone is greeted by first names, there exists the possibility of doing something to help them. However, this also requires a language to communicate in and so many foreigners who come to live here seem unable to speak much Greek beyond *"Kalimera"* and *"Kalispera"*, which mean "Good Morning" and "Good Evening".

Of course, not all the visitors to our Sunday church meetings were struggling and many were just tourists passing through. Thanks to the existence of a local English Paros monthly magazine, *Paros Life*, we were able to place an advertisement informing people of our location and time of our meetings. We never quite knew who would walk through our door on Sundays and it was wonderful to meet such a wide variety of people.

One family of American Missionaries working in Kosovo, who were on holiday on Paros in 2006, were Karl and Jill with their three young children. Another couple, a South African pastor and his wife, Corrie and Carine Du Rand, arrived during the summer months. I remember being so nervous about a pastor being present that I made all kinds of mistakes with the worship and other aspects of the meeting, but he was very gracious and gently encouraged me. Some visitors we never saw again, others we kept in touch with and formed a great network of support and encouragement. It was years later, through Facebook, we discovered that Wencee, our Philippine friend, had become engaged to, and later married, a lovely lady in his church. His first wife had died young, before he came to Paros, which had left him with the task of raising their young daughter alone. Fortunately, his daughter was able to live with his mother while he was working away from home to earn a living to support them.

It was this year, 2006, that God first started to talk to me about house churches being a part of his plan for the future. After more than ten years on Paros, I often prayed about whether we were we ever to grow large enough to need a place to meet outside our home. During my time in Athens at the hospital with Doris, I was able to take a few hours to attend a meeting in the home of a Greek Christian friend where a Dutch man was speaking about groups of Christians meeting in houses. He explained that there were many such groups in Holland and that in India and China, particularly, this is extremely common. I had always thought that the reason God had told me to buy such a large plot of land may have been to build a meeting place on it, but it seemed now that He was telling me that it was not his plan. At some future time of persecution, it could be quite dangerous to meet in public places, and homes would be a much safer place to pray and read the Bible. This theme of meeting in houses had been confirmed by Pastor Corrie Du Rand on his visit to us and, over the years to come, God would repeatedly lead me to the same message to keep me on the right track.

Many times after Sunday meetings, I would cook and try to offer lunch at the house to visitors passing through. At other times we were free to relax. Living on a Greek island we regularly had picnics on the beach, sometimes alone after our Sunday morning meetings, other times with friends who were on holiday. A Greek salad with feta cheese, stuffed vine leaves and delicious big beans in tomato sauce were all we needed for a lovely, simple meal with minimal preparation. If Peter had caught an octopus a few days before, I would steam it until it was tender and that would be an added delicacy to enjoy.

Over the years, we had learned so much about Greek food and the unusual preparation some of it required. In our earlier years on Paros, when the grapes were picked and trampled to make wine, our neighbour, Manolis, would bring us a five-litre container of grape "must". This was the sludge from the bottom of the pit after trampling the grapes. It was a deep, murky, purple colour, but it could be transformed into two kinds of delicious sweets if you were taught how! Manolis had been a chef in the army and loved to bring us things from his small "farm", with instructions on how to use it. If it was milk, it had to be used for rice pudding; tomatoes had to be stuffed; but the grape must, that was another story. First, it had to be boiled in a very large casserole with charcoal, yes, charcoal. The charcoal had to have been used, burnt that is, and then the larger remaining pieces are wrapped in a cloth and tied with string to dangle in the grape must. A miracle then happens. The sludgy mess turns into a crystal clear, purple liquid: the sludge kind of curdles and sinks to the bottom of the pan allowing the clear liquid to be poured off. This is five litres, so more than a gallon of liquid. It then has to be thickened with flour rather like making English gravy. Well, if you need three teaspoons of flour for half a pint of gravy, then for five litres of grape must, that's a lot of flour to be made into a smooth paste, no lumps. Of course, no one ever told me how much flour to use, so I guessed or based it on multiples of three teaspoons. If I got it right, then as I brought the thickened mixture to the boil, I got something like grape blancmange! This then could be poured onto plates to make individual portions, ready to eat or be kept a day or two. For only two people, it would take us about twenty days to eat it all and it would fill the fridge to capacity. The solution is to make "pastilles" which can be kept and eaten throughout the winter months. This is in itself is a three-day job.

First, the thickened grape must is poured about five millimetres thick into large trays, so no roast dinners while this goes on as every metal tray or large plate in the house is being utilised. The trays of must have to stand in the sun to dry out and must be covered with cloths to keep the flies and local cats away. After two or three days, the must becomes rubbery and can be cut into squares. With great patience, each square has to be dipped into sesame seeds and then turned over to dry the other side for another two days. One just has to hope that while all this traditional Parian food preparation is going on, no one falls off their bike and needs to go to hospital: the process must not be interrupted for an untimely trip to Athens!

Our neighbour, Manolis, became a regular visitor to our house. He lived in one large room with a goat pen outside at the back of the house. He had one cold tap for water, no toilet, and was perfectly content. With his chest hair poking over the top of his shirt and sporting a navy cap, he was regularly seen riding his donkey up to the village of Marpissa and back. His wife, Jacomina, lived in a very nice village house with a modern bathroom and kitchen, but Manolis preferred to live in the country with his goats. Jacomina would lovingly prepare his food and Manolis would ride up to their house to collect it. In later years after his donkey died, we would often drive him up to the village as it was too far for him to walk as he got older.

Several of the farmers still rode donkeys around the village and across the fields, but as the years passed the donkey population was getting drastically low. In our early years, it was no problem at all for the community to gather ten or more donkeys for the annual festival of Ascension Day in remembrance of Jesus ascending to heaven fifty days after His resurrection. Young girls in colourful traditional Greek costumes would ride through the harbour at Piso Livadi, the donkeys led by handsome, costumed young boys. Twenty years later, the procession of girls sitting on donkeys had diminished to just one. Most of the donkeys simply died of old age and were never replaced. We did hear of one very funny, but tragic, story of the rather unusual demise of a local donkey. The donkey's owner had a barrel of wine just inside the room where he enjoyed his siesta in the afternoons. Having enjoyed his lunch and lain down to rest, he had failed to notice that the tap on the barrel was slowly dripping wine. Being a rather hot day, even the donkey was in search of some shade at the side of the house. Finding the door ajar and the farmer snoring loudly, the donkey was more than happy to refresh himself by licking up the delicious nectar running down the steps. And he licked and he licked and he licked until he was quite drunk. Freedom seemed a wonderful possibility at that moment and, with the extra courage resulting from the imbibed wine, he leapt across the stone wall and fell and broke his neck. That was another donkey short for the next year's festival!

In later years, Manolis' wife became ill and went to live on Antiparos with their son. No amount of persuasion would get Manolis to join the family, so he then started to cook for himself, needing regular assistance to go to the butcher or supermarket in the village. He rarely seemed to ask the local Greeks or even his brother to take him and we felt very blessed to have him as a neighbour. He accepted us even though we were foreign. Learning to understand his thick Parian accent was quite a challenge though, and we realised just how difficult it was when a Greek visiting from Athens asked us if we could understand him because he couldn't! He was quite impressed when we said we understood at least half of what he said.

Since Manolis chose to live alone, his son decided to install a phone, a tiled shower and toilet, and electricity. At least he could phone and check if he was alright, or he could as long as Manolis hadn't knocked the receiver off the hook, which he often did. The electricity meant that he would be able to have a fridge, TV and light after dark. This was a much safer option than lighting oil lamps, especially after a glass or two of his home-made wine. Even with all these mod cons, it was not at all unusual, when visiting him at home, to find a goat or two in his room with him, especially if the goat had a little one. Sitting on a small stool with a glass of his wine, a chunk of rough cut bread and some excellent strong Parian cheese, this was an experience not to be missed. We considered ourselves quite privileged to know him.

When Manolis died many years later in the summer of 2013, I was in England attending a forty year student reunion in Manchester and visiting family. He had been perfectly healthy when I left, so had died with none of the pain and suffering of sickness. Peter only found out the day after the funeral that he had died. It is one of the many frustrations of life in Greece where funerals occur within 24–48 hours after death. If you live outside the village, you may not see the poster announcing the funeral unless it happens to be a shopping day! We used to get upset that no one phoned and told us, but we learnt that it was just Greek life so not to take it personally. It was not because we are foreigners; even the locals have the same problem.

Another aspect of life on a Greek island is entertaining visitors. When you live in an environment that feels close to paradise during the summer months, it is hardly surprising that a constant stream of visitors passes through, some staying at the house and some in rooms nearby. As well as the challenge of planning menus for their one to three week visit, there is the dilemma of what exactly do you do every day with people who have come expressly to visit you? They want to see the island, go to the beach, relax in cafés and eat in local tavernas. For the resident, the challenge is to do all these things, plus the shopping, cooking, washing, ironing and gardening, while maintaining an air of calm relaxation and being available from morning until bedtime!

It was on such a morning, during an annual visit from my niece, that I suggested we go to Farangas beach on the south side of the island. It should have been an ordinary day at the beach, but it just seems that extraordinary things happen to me all the time.

We arrived early around 11a.m. to see a beautiful luxury motor launch moored in the bay. It was fairly quiet; most of the late night party people hadn't stirred yet. I settled down under a tree at the back of the beach, planning to write to my friend Doris. Tracy chose a pole position in full sun next to the shoreline. The next thing we knew, two uniformed crew from the motor launch arrived on the beach in a large speed boat. They set up eight beach chairs complete with umbrellas, towels, sun tan lotion and a cool box for drinks. About half an hour later the guests arrived: mostly couples with some children, definitely Australian from the accent. I felt that I should finish the letter later and go down to the water's edge near to them, so I went over to Tracy, laid my towel down and plunged into the water to cool down. A man, who could have been the captain, came over and asked us if they were disturbing us.

"No, not at all, it's rather interesting to see the cruiser."

He offered us two cold beers which we accepted just to be friendly and, in return, I thought to offer my book to the lady on the end of the row of chairs. Her name was

Sandy. She immediately started to read it and another man, who overheard us talking, came over and said,

"We heard about an English lady that lived on Paros and had left her job in England, while we were staying in Athens. That must be you!"

Possibly they had met another Australian couple that I had been talking to on Paros. They asked where they could get more books so I gave her a second copy which I had with me and showed her my email address.

As they left an hour later and returned to their cruiser, I realised the series of events required for that meeting to take place. Firstly, Tracy had to be staying with me or else I would never have been on the beach at that time of day and I rarely went to that particular beach. Secondly, we had originally planned to go to lunch in Aliki first and then to the beach, but we changed our minds. Thirdly, our car (the Subaru) was overheating and if our friends Jean and Barry hadn't already left the island and left us the use of their car, we would have stayed closer to home and not been there at all. Fourthly, the schedule of the cruiser had to include a stop on a relatively small beach on its way from Santorini and Serifos before continuing on to Mykonos. Fifthly, the captain needed to offer the beer for me to have the opening to offer my book and, finally, they had to be in the right place in Athens to meet the couple who knew me. If that wasn't a God appointment I don't know what was!

The place Peter and I would more usually be sitting was at Gregory's café at the far end of Logaras. It was on such a day in 2006 that we made a rather impulsive decision that was to directly affect our freedom in the coming years. As we were sitting enjoying a cool drink after the heat of the day, Anna Fisilani from the taverna next door walked by holding a gorgeous, white puppy, only a few weeks old. When our previous dog Abee had died at about fifteen years of age, we had decided that we wouldn't have another dog. It was too painful a loss when they died and it does have a significant impact on daily life, walking them, training them to behave appropriately with visitors, and so on. Travelling anywhere required prior arrangements with neighbours or friends to feed and exercise the dog, which created a mounting sense of indebtedness since it was never on a paid for basis.

I had always thought that if we ever did change our minds, I would like to have a white dog, probably a Labrador, as they are so gentle and good with children. In spite of all this, we still asked Anna if she wanted a home for the little fellow, but she was quite insistent, no, she wanted to keep the puppy. He was one of a litter of ten puppies which had been found dumped in a box on the Logaras car park. This is not such an uncommon occurrence in Greece. Homes had been found for all ten, but one lady, Roula, had taken two simply because they needed a home. Anna suggested that if we went to ask her, she might be prepared to give one away. We were so excited to go and see them that we rushed off that same evening instead of praying about it beforehand.

Roula had been our neighbour during the two years we had lived in the village. On arrival at her home, we found her daughter playing with the two puppies. They both looked much the same, both male and mostly black, and, yes, her mother would be happy to let us have one. As I chose one, the little girl said, "Oh no, not that one, he's my mum's favourite", so I gladly changed him for the other one and off we went. It was like the joy I had felt when I first took Abee home all over again, so small, sweet and helpless. While he was a puppy, he became a regular part of my quiet time as I read my Bible with the dog nestling at my feet. I took him to the beach with me, using the same scarf I had used for Abee fifteen years before to strap him against my chest. Everyone loved him, especially the children. Pavlos and Mariana, two children living locally for the school holidays, waited for him to arrive every day. They then would play with him on the beach for hours. We decided to call him Sam, a popular name for dogs in England. To me, it came from the name Samuel, which means "I asked the Lord for him", and was a reference to Hannah in the Old Testament who was childless and asked the Lord for a son. I had asked the Lord if we could have another little dog quite some time before finding this one.

It wasn't all fun and games though. After we had settled Sam in for a few weeks, we thought it would be okay to leave him on his own for a few hours while we went out to dinner with friends. We put him in the West Wing on his bed and closed the door so he wouldn't run off. Amongst the many things stored in the West Wing was a wall unit, normally in the main house but, in the summer, we would move it out of the dining room to make room for three beds in there for our visitors. If Peter's mum came with two of his sisters, we needed three beds for them to sleep. The dining room could easily be converted into a bedroom for the summer months as we always ate outside on the veranda.

The wall units had glass shelves and the best crystal wine glasses were kept in there. I never dreamt it was likely to cause a problem. He was a tiny puppy, the wall units were two metres high and the lower doors were made of wood, not glass. We arrived home around 10p.m. As we stepped into the storage room, glass crunched under our feet. We turned on the light to find a scene of utter destruction and a poor, terrified little Sam trembling from head to foot. We worked out that Sam was upset at being left alone for the first time and had jumped up at the door to try to get out. The problem was he was just a little guy so he didn't know which door to jump at. Probably, he had jumped up at the wall units and the glass shelf, held on by thirty-year-old plastic clips, had collapsed. The cut glass wine goblets had cascaded to the ground, no doubt with a deafening crash to the ears of a little puppy. I rushed in to pick up little Sam, checking his paws to see if he was bleeding. By some miracle he was not cut. Somehow it didn't seem to matter that the glasses were gone, even if they were very expensive Stuart crystal. It was a part of my life that was over and they were rather ostentatious on a Greek island, where many people used cheap Pyrex glasses anyway. For sure I wouldn't be replacing them with similar crystal glasses.

It was only years later, as Sam grew into an adult dog, that we realised he looked exactly the same as Abee did apart from being a different colour. He had the same nose, eyes and beard, the same wiry hair and was about the same size. After two years without a dog, I had told God that I really didn't want a Labrador or a Spaniel, I just wanted a dog like Abee again, I missed him so much. Well here he was, and his brother that I had first chosen looked nothing like him. Sam was the one of the ten puppies that was a typical Griffon, or 'Wirehaired Pointing Griffon' to be exact. Sam never did have quite the same gentle character as Abee. He was much more dominant by nature and quite a handful to control at times. Every time someone came to the house to visit, he was so pleased to see them that he would sit next to them throughout their visit or, worse still, prostrate himself across their lap. Even for those who liked dogs, it was a bit too much affection. For many Greeks, who just weren't used to the idea of a dog being a part of the family and living indoors, it didn't work too well at all. There was nothing to do but put Sam outside in the West Wing and leave him to voice his protest. When the visitors left, he was allowed to rush gleefully back inside the house again.

September came with a bang: the first rain arrived with a terrific thunder storm and lightning bolts bounced between Paros and Naxos. Helen and John, our Greek/Australian friends, had also arrived to spend some time in their home in Naoussa. John had been born on Paros and, having left as a young man to find work in Australia, he had met and married Helen, an indigenous

Australian of Aboriginal descent. Initially, he had worked building roads across the desert in the blazing sun. They now had grown up children in Australia so were never likely to live full time on Paros, but John still had some of his brothers and sisters living here. During their visits, they always joined our Sunday meetings, but we had no midweek meetings at that time. Helen suggested that, while John worked in their garden and fixed things around the house, she would be free to join us for a midweek prayer meeting. At this point in my walk with God, prayer meetings were not an attractive prospect. I found the idea of a shopping list of prayer requests to bring before God rather tedious; I needed someone to teach me that there was far more to prayer than just this.

We started to meet in the main town so that the other ladies would not have to travel over the mountains to our side twice a week. Lornie had a second-hand book shop, and during the afternoon siesta time it was closed so we could use it as a place to pray. Slowly, as the weeks passed, we learnt how to enter into the presence of God through worship and then to bring not just our requests before God, but our thanks, our questions and our every need to just feel His love. Prior to all this, group prayer had been minimal on Sundays and prayer was just whatever we did as individuals throughout the week. Now, we would begin to learn the power of corporate prayer, the increased power of a praying group, rather than just individual prayer. For Helen, prayer was what she was called to do. Over the years she had gradually released herself from the many other church activities to spend more time seeking God. I, on the other hand, spent a lot time working for God, evangelizing, teaching on Sundays, but not nearly enough time seeking His presence and His strategy through prayer. As the years passed, the emphasis changed and prayer and God's presence became everything to me.

Initially, our core group of prayer ladies was Lornie, Swiss Annamarie and me. Some Christians on holiday here would find out about the prayer meetings through the bookshop and we welcomed others to join us. For some reason unknown to us, we rarely had a man join us for prayer. It was not that they were unwelcome, they just rarely came. It was as if they felt that prayer was something women did, while they got on with the practical things of life. Later, when Lornie left the island, Jenny from New Zealand joined the group and we had our core three back again.

12 A SPECIAL FAREWELL

I was sitting outside on the West Wing terrace. It was a pleasantly warm October day, not at all like the intense heat of August where one moves progressively from the shade of a tree to the more substantial cover of a bamboo pergola, finally crawling indoors to the relative cool of the bedroom. The birds were chirping happily in the bougainvillea, content to find worms at last, in the newly turned soil. Tassos, our neighbour's son, had turned out the well-rested plough, eager to chew through the flat, scorched fields bereft of even a blade of grass after five months without a drop of rain.

The rain on Paros was late in 2007, even though all over mainland Greece there had been rain for weeks, and when it came the thirsty fire-scorched land drank in the desperately needed water. Acres and acres of burnt forest had left the once beautiful Peloponnese a black, scarred mass of burnt stumps. For weeks the clouds had teased us, promising to rain, and then had left the land as dry and dusty as when they had blown in. Finally, the much prayed for downpour had arrived. As we lay in bed, the torrents lashed against the simple roof of beams and bamboo. The

West Wing was in the more traditional style of construction on Paros and all the Cycladic islands, unlike the earthquake resilient concrete frame of the main house. Both of the rooms opened directly outside, so, knowing that the whole toilet and shower area would be awash from the sudden rush of water, a trip to the bathroom in the night would be deferred as long as possible. This wasn't the gentle, soft, steady rain we wanted to coax the thirsty soil to drink, but a deluge cascading off the white boards of the pergola which had sheltered us all summer long from the ferocious heat. Our dog, Sam, and our tiny, twelve week old, black and white kitten, Alexis, nestled together on the cushion at the foot of our bed, warm and secure, unlike the many stray cats outdoors seeking a place of refuge from this strange, wet stuff falling from the sky. Our visitors in the main house were far better protected from the rain than we were.

It should have been a happy and peaceful day, yet there was a heaviness hanging over me knowing that my mum had been lying in a hospital bed, a thousand miles away in England, for thirty-eight days. She had an abscess on the colon/rectum – well, somewhere down there in the sewage system of the body. She was eighty-six years old and had a weak heart since a full heart bypass more than fifteen years earlier; the doctors were reluctant to perform surgery with a general anaesthetic. Twice, they had tried to drain the abscess externally and, medically, her chances of success for a normal operation were slim.

I arranged a phone call direct to the ward where mum was, at a prearranged time when my sister would be there to organise the practicalities of taking the call.

"Hi Mum, it's Barbara." It was good to hear her voice at last as she was often asleep, sedated for the pain from the abscess with morphine. Now she was completely conscious. First of all, I told her how much I loved her and that we were praying for her to be up and out of that place. Then I moved the conversation to some forgiveness issues that needed to be dealt with to ensure that nothing was blocking her healing. After talking with her, it was clear that she had dealt with everything necessary; it was such a relief to hear it.

Even so, she still didn't seem to respond to prayer and be well enough to leave the hospital. I was torn between my responsibilities on Paros and my responsibility to her. She really had been in hospital for an excessively long time. Finally, I felt the Lord released me to go to visit her and I flew into England on a Tuesday in November. The very next day, I went to the hospital armed with a small bottle of oil and my Bible. I felt that I was supposed to anoint her with oil and pray the prayer of faith in the book of James. I had God's promise that the prayer offered in faith would make the sick person well.

On arrival, I was shocked to see Mum curled up on the hospital bed in a foetal position, nothing but skin and bone. I had asked the doctor if there was any plan to discharge her that week, to which he firmly replied, "No chance, maybe next week". They always try to give people hope. I gently explained to Mum that I wanted to pray with her and she responded, "Oh that would be lovely". I then read the passage from the book of James and anointed her with oil. In the next two hours she recovered enough to ask to get out of bed and sit in a chair. Two days later, that same week, she was miraculously well enough to be discharged, in spite of the doctor's original negative response. After more than a month in hospital, one prayer was all it had taken to raise her up.

We got her safely settled into the residential care home where Margaret had taken her clothes, photographs and personal items to make it seem more homely. Each day of my stay I visited her for several hours and was thrilled to see her on her feet again, walking from room to room. The comparison to how she had barely shuffled from bed to chair in the hospital was marked. There were daily recreational activities and physiotherapy once a week to limber up all the old joints and strengthen their muscles. It was all done as a program of games with sponge balls and sticks to get them moving. The staff had a gift of getting the most reluctant residents to join in and helping them as necessary. Finally, I felt satisfied that, as residential homes went, she was in one where she could, perhaps, be happy and enjoy the company of others. She had been very lonely where she had lived before and was no longer capable of living alone.

It was just four days to my return flight home to Paros. After a pleasant morning with Mum and lunch with the other residents in the dining room, it seemed an ideal opportunity to pop into town to do a bit of Christmas shopping. I would be able to find everyone much better presents in England than on Paros and, since I wouldn't have to post them, I'd have more flexibility to buy some bulkier items. It was a novel experience for me to wander around the large indoor shopping centre in Wolverhampton and, even though it was still November, the shops were in full swing for Christmas. Beaties, the local department store, looked like a fairy castle to me after the small shops of Paros, the lights twinkling in the dark as I came out laden with packages. I was all set to catch the bus back to Mum's flat where I was staying.

I hadn't been home more than a few minutes when the phone rang; it was my nephew. The residential home had rung to say that Mum had had a fall. She seemed fine, but they just wanted to notify us. Unfortunately, by 1p.m. the next day, they had rung again to say that she had been taken to hospital to be checked over. Margaret and I were just about ready to go over to the home to visit her when the call came through, so there was nothing to do but wait until they brought her back. We waited and waited but the second call to confirm her return never came. It seemed best to drive over to the hospital, a journey Margaret had hoped to never have to make again. We tracked mum down in the emergency area, only to be informed that she had broken her hip and would need a full hip replacement if she was ever to walk again. It was scheduled for the next morning.

We decided to go to church and leave her in God's hands. There was nothing we could do there. By the time we finished our worship meeting, the operation would be over. They gave her only a fifty-fifty chance of survival due to her weak heart and her age. I had no wish to see her struggle on any more. She was unhappy, worn-out and tired and only wanted to die and go to heaven to be with Dad. I found myself weeping at the end of the Sunday service when someone asked how Mum was. I was convinced she was about to die and that I would never see her again. It was as if our Friday lunch had been our last meal together.

Well, it almost was our last meal together. Mum did pull through the operation, but was totally confused after it. She was unable to grasp where she was, why her leg hurt and why had they not brought her breakfast or lunch. She had of course had both, but her life was becoming a jumble to her and all too much of an effort. She struggled on for another three weeks. The hospital indicated she could go on for anything from two weeks to three months as she was; her skin was oozing liquid as her kidneys were failing and she had caught yet another hospital infection. This time, I didn't feel I was supposed to pray for her healing. She was miserable and she just wanted to die. She had long since lost the will to live on without Dad; it seemed best just to pray for the Lord to take her home if it was her time to go.

By the time she died in December, I was back on Paros. Not knowing how long she would hang on for, I had taken my flight back home as scheduled. Peter was more than ready to have me back home and my sister was at her side daily. The funeral was arranged for the 28th. I would fly to England again two days earlier. I knew it was the end of an era; one phase of my life was over; I no longer had a mum or dad. Although I felt very sad about losing her, I also felt a tremendous relief. It had always been difficult to answer Mum's question, "Do you think you will ever come back to live in England?"

After years of sacrifice bringing up her two children, she had always expected to have us both close by when she grew old. Like most mothers, she had longed for grandchildren and great grandchildren, but I had never given her any. Fortunately, she had two grandchildren from Margaret. I felt it was unlikely that I would ever return to England; God had put me in Greece and I certainly had no desire to return. It seemed improbable to me that He would move me back to England, and I actually felt rather blessed to have been given the opportunity to leave!

13 CANCER AGAIN

It all started somewhere around the end of October 2009. The summer was coming to an end and my sister and her daughter had just left after their annual summer visit. I felt that I needed some time away from the remaining tourists and just wanted to be quiet. I was desperate to spend some time with God and Peter was happy enough to let me have some time to myself. I decided to spend ten days alone, separated from the normal day to day things of life. Peter could cook for himself without any problem. During these days, I spent much of my time reading my Bible and meditating on God's word. Many times my thoughts would turn to God's promise of the restoration of my breast. Fifteen years had passed, since the ship *Restoration* had sailed into Piraeus harbour the very day I had prayed for restoration.

Some ladies on the island had informed me that the new mammogram equipment at the Paros health centre was now in operation following a considerable delay to find an operator. One might have thought that a hospital post on a Greek island would be an attractive proposition compared to life in the chaos of Athens, but it would seem not. Most young medics are drawn to big hospitals with better facilities and better career prospects. The poor salaries and the need to pay rent for accommodation also made Paros economically unattractive. In Athens, most of them had family they could live with.

Several of my friends had made appointments and, for some reason, I decided I would go, too. After all, it was fifteen years since my operation and, normally, an annual mammogram would be a minimum requirement. Since I was so sure I was healed, I'd never really thought much about check-ups. I thought that it would be a good opportunity to confirm to everyone I was healed. With hindsight, I had always said that if I believe I am healed, why go for a check-up: wouldn't that be a demonstration of doubt?

The result turned out to be not what I had been expecting at all. The doctor had circled a suspect area and I was advised to go to the mammography department of a large cancer hospital in Athens, *Agios Savvas*, (Saint Savvas). While it caused me some concern to receive the news, I felt sure it was just lumpy breast tissue, as a doctor had told me two years previously when I had had blood tests and a physical examination.

Before I made an appointment at the hospital, I received a call from a Christian friend in Glyfada. She told me that Benny Hinn, an international evangelist, would be in Athens on 11 November. Anna was going to the meeting with her church and would be really pleased if I would stay with her. It seemed ideal to book a hospital appointment for the day before and then go to the Benny Hinn meeting the next day. Perhaps, after the doctors had examined me and seen that I had only one breast, this would be the time for my restoration. Peter couldn't understand why I was so excited about the restoration of my left breast; all he wanted was the lump in my right breast sorted out.

I arranged to stay with Poppy and Thomas the first

night. They had just had their long-awaited first child. When they had been on Paros for the summer holidays, we had not had much time together, everyone trying to do the daily domestic jobs before midday and then sleeping in the midday heat. She picked me up from the ferry and brought me to their home. As we chatted, I told her it was nothing to worry about. I was focused on the Benny Hinn meeting, Jesus and my restoration.

No one was more surprised than me when, on examination, the doctor, an elderly man with years of experience, told me it was a tumour and it was cancer. I suggested that we should at least remain optimistic until we had the biopsy. After all, aren't eighty percent of breast tumours benign? Yes, he agreed that they were, but an hour later we had the results and he was right, it was cancer again. I just couldn't understand it. Every day for fifteen years, Peter and I, when saying grace before our meals, had thanked God for my healing and said that "by Jesus' wounds I have been healed". "In Jesus' name, the cancer will never come back". When I was finally alone outside the hospital, I spoke authoritatively to my body and commanded any cancer to be gone in Jesus' name.

Returning to Poppy's home, it absolutely poured down. I had hoped to do some Christmas shopping but, with the rain and my spirits dampened by the doctor's bad report, I wasn't really in the mood. At a street kiosk, I found a perfect, small, leather bag which was exactly what my sister wanted and abandoned the rest of the shopping.

After lunch with Poppy, we decided an afternoon nap would be good for all of us. I lay on the bed by the long, sliding glass windows onto the terrace and looked at the sky. The sun had broken through even though it was still raining and a beautiful rainbow arched the skies. What a reminder of God's covenant promises to me. He was my healer, deliverer and Saviour and He had promised He would never leave me. He had also sent his servant, Benny Hinn, to Greece at just the right time to minister to me.

The next day I set off at midday; I wanted to be there well before the crowds arrived, even though the start of the meeting was only 7p.m. The doors were due to open at five, but I expected people to start queuing early and wanted to be there at 2:30p.m. It was a long walk down some very steep slopes to the train station and I didn't know the way too well. Then, at the other end, it was quite a walk from the station. Any ideas of wearing a smart suit had to be abandoned; it would have to be jeans and trainers for comfort as well as to hide my money in my socks. Athens was crawling with thieves and pick-pockets. Boy, did I feel under-dressed on arrival; everyone else was wearing their best suit, or a smart dress.

Much to my amazement, they did have my name on the list of attendees and I was escorted to the third row from the front. I had been told a week earlier, when I had tried to book, that the minimum group size for booking was fifteen. God had gone before me. All afternoon, as technicians worked on the sound and ushers checked the seating, I was able to sit quietly praying for what God would do. I could feel heat all over my breasts, neck and head: the Holy Spirit was already working in my body. By 4p.m., the doors had been closed to the crowds gathering outside, and I seemed to be the only non-staff member in the place. I was left to bask in the presence of God. By the time the meeting started, my faith was high and I was ready for anything God had in mind to do.

After the worship and the preaching, Benny Hinn asked for those who could feel God healing their bodies to come forward. I was up like a shot and circled the arena to reach the queue formed on the other side. The usher asked what I had been healed of.

"Well, I was diagnosed yesterday with a tumour in my breast and now I can feel heat all over my breasts." I was projected to the front of the queue and, before I knew it, I was the first one on stage. I repeated the statement I had made about the diagnosis and the heat all over my breasts.

Before I could say anything about my other breast and the promise of restoration through the sign of the ship, I fell to the ground when Benny Hinn prayed for me. I remember being pulled up once by the catchers and then being back on the floor, so it seemed a good opportunity to check my breast. I couldn't feel the tumour at all as I felt through my clothes, carefully moving my fingers around the lower part of the breast where it had been.

"It's gone", I exclaimed, and Benny Hinn laughed and replied, "I am sure it's gone". And that was it! They moved on to the next person and, rejoicing, I walked back to my seat. I was so relieved that the tumour was gone. Then, to my horror, I could feel it again. Had it gone and come back because I was checking it was gone? No, that's ridiculous. I was just confirming it was gone. I had learnt enough to know not to change my confession of healing to one of doubt. Now, I would have to believe in: "The God who ... calls the things that are not as though they were" Romans 4.

People at the end of the meeting came up to me and remarked: "How marvellous, praise God you got your healing!" In my mind I didn't feel healed, and the battle had begun. The word of God says I am healed. As I walked up the street with Anna, I was very quiet. Now, I would have to see if I really believed what I had been teaching for fifteen years about believing before you see it.

Every day for the next month, I prayed healing scriptures, thanking God for my healing even though the lump was still evident. I knew that the hospital would phone me about a month after my biopsy, so I felt I had to get the manifestation of the healing before they called. Peter was insistent that if the lump had not gone by the time they phoned, I had to go and be operated on. If only I could have got the threat of the hospital phone call off my mind, it would have been much easier to rest in prayer. I felt under terrific pressure.

On exactly 11 December, the hospital rang to call me

for an operation. I just couldn't go through with it; I was so sure I had been healed, feeling all that heat over me in the Benny Hinn meeting then genuinely believing the lump was gone. It couldn't have all been for nothing. I told the lady on the phone that I was taking another therapy for my healing, (meaning Jesus and prayer), and that I couldn't come now. She, of course, thought that I meant treatment at another hospital. She asked what I wanted to do, so I said, "Put me down for January". I was thinking that, by then, the lump would have gone and the operation would be cancelled, but I probably should have said, "Call me back in January". Words are very important and Mark 11 says: "What he says will happen. It will be done for him".

Now, of course, I had to tell Peter what I had done. I was feeling very guilty because he had said I had to go when they phoned me. Throughout lunch, I said nothing. I took the dog for his regular walk although it was raining. I didn't feel free now, even though the hospital was off my back, I just felt guilty. I was expecting Peter to be really mad with me. I would have to tell him they'd phoned.

I started with, "Peter, I have to tell you something! The hospital rang today and I told them I wasn't ready." I was right, he was angry!

"And how long do you think you are going to wait before . . ."

In the end, I agreed I would call the hospital back and see what they had done with my response. Though it was rather late, and I had no extension number to call, I was transferred to the correct office. It seemed they had booked me down for a call on 10 January. With that, Peter seemed appeased. Now, I had time to pray and wait on God. God had made a way to give me the time I needed to receive the physical manifestation of the healing. The lump would disappear and I would not need an operation.

Every Sunday in the weeks that followed, I taught about faith, healing, the principle of praising God before seeing our miracle, giving victory shouts of triumph in battle and the healing power of Jesus in taking the bread and wine of Communion. A wonderful peace descended on me after the mental turmoil of the previous month. Yet that living personal "rhema" word of God just never came. A "rhema" word is a living, active word which comes into being. "Rhema" in Greek is a verb; it is an utterance, a thing spoken. The days slipped by; Christmas came and went, and 10 January was rapidly approaching.

Looking back, my problem was that, at that time, I only believed for a supernatural removal of the lump. T.L. Osborne, a great evangelist with a healing ministry, points out that one of the reasons some people fail to receive their healing at all is that they discount God healing through natural and medical means and are only looking for a supernatural healing. That was probably my problem at this time. God would explain to me why He was allowing all this to happen but not for a while yet.

The hospital call duly came and I meekly accepted their offer of a bed for an operation. Lornie had offered to travel up with me and see me through the maze of Greek paperwork that goes with hospital admittance. I still believed that I would receive a last minute reprieve and that the lump would disappear and the operation would be cancelled. I suspect it was more hope than faith.

By the time we arrived at the *Agios Savvas* hospital, all faith had evaporated and I felt like a frightened rabbit. That was an expression used by Yonngi Cho, the pastor of the world's largest church in Korea. He had prayed for two months for finances to build a church and the money just hadn't come through. As the payment deadline approached, he said he had felt like a frightened rabbit! For him, his breakthrough came at the three month mark. For me, time had almost run out.

The hospital room looked brand new. It was in a new wing and had only four beds in it, plus a private bathroom. I was the first to arrive – the other beds were unoccupied – but, as I settled in, another three ladies joined me. We were all scheduled for a batch of pre-operation tests. This required negotiating long corridors and stairways, with instructions given in Greek, to find funny-sounding department names. For two days, it was checks on my blood, my heart, and bone scans. I was injected with a radioactive liquid and shown to a small room with a toilet where I was instructed to drink one and a half litres of water. The others in the room talked of their remorse over the three packets of cigarettes they had smoked every day and the coffee they had drunk. What they thought coffee had to do with cancer, I failed to see. They commented, "If only I had known, but I was young then", as if that was an excuse for all their previous misdemeanours and ignorance.

I took the opportunity to point out that while cigarettes were a factor, it was also important, at a time like this, to ask God's forgiveness for any sin in our life, especially for having cut off anyone through unforgiveness. This was a particularly common occurrence in families in Greece. It was essential that we all asked God to forgive any sin in our lives which may have opened the door to sickness. Initially, this was a bit of a conversation stopper, and one man commented that he thought it unwise to be too extreme in our religion. At this point, the arrival of another elderly gentleman certainly picked up the conversation. He began to talk of all the immoral relationships he had had as a young man, but he was young then so that was okay! However, to be living like that when someone was fifty, that would be a sin! I smiled inwardly at how people make excuses for their behaviour, as if sin is not sin when you are young but it would be after fifty. I left them talking as I was called to go to the scanner, my one and a half litres of water duly consumed. As I lay down on the flat bed for a perfectly painless examination, I was overwhelmed with a total sense of failure and tears streamed down my face. All I believed, all I had taught, had it really come to this?

When, three days later, the surgeon visited me, almost

as an afterthought I asked him if he had the scan results. "Oh yes, everything's fine", he said. So all the tests were fine, the cancer had not spread anywhere else in my body and was localised in the tumour. There was still time for a miracle!

Lornie and I had no idea when I was scheduled for my operation. The lady in the next bed had come in, had been operated on and had left two days later. It seemed that I was stuck there for the weekend. Well, perhaps it wasn't so bad. The lady who had just left was a school teacher from another island. I had been reading a booklet in Greek about Jesus healing and had given her the same booklet to read the first day that we were both hospitalised. The next day, I was interested to know if she had read any of the sixty pages, so I said something about believing in our healing before seeing it. I said that, with cancer, it wasn't just the healing of the breast but of the whole body, but that perhaps she had not read that far in the book.

"Oh yes", she said, "I read the whole book through last night!" A prayer to receive Christ was on page four and she had prayed it to receive Christ as her Saviour believing, as she did, in Jesus as the Son of God. She taught 6–12-year-old children and, in Greece, that includes Religious Instruction.

On the Friday morning, stalking the hospital corridor in the hope of finding the surgeon on his rounds, we managed to find out that I was scheduled for operation on Tuesday morning. Operations were only performed on Tuesdays, Wednesdays and Thursdays so that was the next available slot. Storm force winds were forecast for the weekend, so it was impossible for me to travel back to Paros and return on Monday. It seemed best for Lornie to travel back before the storm, and I would take the opportunity of some quality time alone with God. All the other ladies were either finished or had places to stay in Athens for the weekend, so I would be quite alone. I decided not to take up the offer to stay with Poppy in

Piraeus. I wasn't feeling too sociable so better to stay where I was and to be quiet with God. I really didn't mind, I was ready for some peace and quiet. I had my worship music on an MP3 player, together with thirty half-hour teachings on the theme "God Wants You Well". The food was exceptionally good for a hospital, two cooked meals a day: chicken and roast potatoes, oven baked fish, spaghetti Bolognese and Greek *pastichio* were just some of the meals I had, all served with a healthy salad, fruit and yoghurt.

A big surprise was to come at the weekend. Helen and John from Australia walked through the door to pray for me and to encourage me. With their daughter just starting a new job in Switzerland in the autumn, they had decided on a trip to Switzerland and to Greece, so they were here just when I needed their support. I explained to Helen the verses from Psalms that I had been given: Psalm 124:7–8: "We have escaped like a bird out of the fowler's snare, the snare has been broken . . . Our help is in the name of the Lord". As I spoke, the presence of God was very strong and I experienced those all too familiar goose bumps from my head to my waist as we sat on the bed chatting.

Since I would be in Athens on the Sunday, it was an ideal opportunity to visit Liberis' church for a full Sunday meeting. John and Helen kindly offered to come too, even though calling at the hospital to collect me was not the easiest route for them. It would be an opportunity to worship and pray together, and to ensure that I had dealt with all the spirits of infirmity and cancer that needed to be expelled. Before the meeting even started, Liberis took the opportunity to teach me again on the difference between faith and hope. I thought I was well aware of the difference and he told me that only with faith, not just hope alone, could I receive my healing. It was less than encouraging, having him tell me that I clearly didn't have faith or else I would have received the manifestation of my healing. The strange thing was that, although I wasn't sure that the tumour would be removed supernaturally without an operation, I had never doubted for a minute that I was healed of cancer and that the rest of my body was fine. Other friends with cancer talked in fear about uncertainty of the future, whether they would live. I knew I would live, I just didn't know what path the healing would take. Would it be supernatural, or would it be at the hands of a surgeon?

Actually I should have known, because right at the beginning of November while on Paros, the Lord had spoken to me as I sat praying on a rock in the mountains around Spring Valley. I had heard that inner voice tell me that I had to go for an operation because there were two people that were to be saved. If I didn't go to hospital, they would be lost. I was now sure the school teacher was one of the two. No doubt, the next week, I would find out who was the second one, and I certainly did find out.

Christina was a Greek lady in the bed opposite. I had first seen her on the Friday morning before Lornie had left. She looked very afraid and had dark rings under her eyes, looking frail and tired. They had shown her to her bed, but she had left to spend the weekend with family in Athens. She lived on the mainland of Greece some 200 Kilometres from Athens. On Monday, she returned for various tests and decided she would stay at the hospital; I would again have some company. The ladies allocated to the other two beds lived close by and wouldn't use their beds until after their operation. For Monday night, it would just be Christina and I.

We chatted a little bit during the day. Peter had travelled up to be with me and Christina's husband was with her. It was only after the men left and we had changed into our pyjamas for the night that we really got into conversation. Peter was sleeping at the Athens house of Marouso, our neighbour on Logaras. I told Christina that I believed in Jesus doing miracles and that I had not expected to need an operation, which then opened the door for her to tell me of two healings that she had received through prayer. She had had a growth on her head and had been anointed with oil from a particular monastery and the lump had gone. On a later occasion, she had a sore on her foot, in between her toes, which would not heal and doctors had failed to find any cure. The leg had swollen to a massive size right up to her knee. Again, she had been anointed with oil and her leg and foot were completely healed. Being Greek, she gave the glory for the healings to the saints of the churches where the oil came from. This was a perfect opportunity for me to explain to her that it was Jesus who died on the cross for our forgiveness and healing, not any of the saints. In the New Testament book of James where, in the church, we are instructed to anoint the sick with oil in the name of the Lord for healing, it is quite clear that the healing comes from Jesus not from any saint, man or woman. I explained that it was Jesus who had healed her and that we must give Him the glory. She understood perfectly and did not disagree in any way. She then went to her bag and brought a book of handwritten prayers to show me. The prayers were written in large letters with black felt tip pen as she had very poor eyesight. I opened the Greek booklet written by Liberis and showed her the special prayer to receive Christ as her Saviour and healer. Since the print was too small for her to read herself, I read each line aloud and she prayed it after me. As if to be sure she wouldn't forget what she had prayed, she then carefully wrote it out word for word in her precious little prayer book. We hugged and kissed and then I explained more to her. We asked Jesus to heal our breasts and her eyesight, so that she would be able to read the Bible. If I had heard Jesus correctly that day at Spring Valley, I had just shown the second of the two the way to salvation. If this was why Jesus had chosen the hospital route to healing and not the supernatural route, then that was okay with me.

Peter arrived early the next morning, cold and tired. The apartment where he had stayed had been unheated and empty for weeks. It was bitterly cold outside. They dressed, or rather undressed me for surgery and my bed had already been remade with clean sheets. This was a big improvement on the hospital fifteen years earlier which couldn't even give me clean sheets days after my operation. The trolley was finally wheeled into the room.

"Barbara Gilis?"

"Yes, that's me."

I resigned myself to the inevitable operation. I must have looked a strange sight being wheeled into the operating theatre clutching a piece of A4 paper with a message for the surgeon written in Greek and English: "LUMP ONLY, NOT ALL THE BREAST!"

I wasn't taking any chances. The surgeon had visited us the day before and asked if I wanted the whole breast removed or just the lump/tumour? What a question! I thought doctors decided such things on the basis of their experience, but it seemed that times had changed since my first operation in 1994. I had been pretty upset then that they had removed the whole breast without asking me; at least now I was being given the choice. Medically, I knew that some people consider the removal of the whole breast a safer option in order to prevent any re-occurrence of tumours. But I had had the experience of a full mastectomy, the whole breast removed, the disfigurement of my body, the agony in my arm resulting from the loss of lymph glands and muscle. The alternative of removing just the lump would be an easier path. I had gone to the hospital stairwell to be alone to pray and to make my decision. It was the only place where I could be alone. Which option would I choose? Did God have a preference; was one better than the other? I thought, "Well, what if it was a lump on my leg and he had said I could either have my leg cut off below the knee or just the lump removed". Clearly, just the lump would be my choice. I was confident I was healed anyway. I would be fine with only the removal of the tumour. Decided, I went back to the ward, told Peter my decision and waited for the surgeon to return, but he never came.

The day passed, the morning of the operation arrived and still I had had no chance to communicate my decision to the surgeon or anyone else.

"What if they put me under the anaesthetic before I can tell them? I will be devastated if I wake up and they have removed my right breast as well!"

So that was the background to how it came about that I was clutching my "lump only sign" as they loaded me off the trolley and through the serving hatch into the operating area like a Sunday roast chicken waiting to be carved. I lay waiting in the corridor as six or more separate teams were operating in as many operating theatres. What an amazing place. As they wheeled one out, it was my turn.

"Oh God, why all this?" I asked, but I suppose He had already told me. Several of the team were already present. The anaesthetist had trained in England and we chatted away in English as she hooked me up to various pieces of equipment. Yes, she would make sure that the surgeon knew it was just a lumpectomy, not a full radical surgery, not the removal of the whole breast. And that was it! I remembered nothing more until it was all over and they were wheeling me back to my bed. I slept and dozed for the afternoon and then, much to my amazement, nurses came to dress me and get me out of bed to walk about. My word, times had changed! Nurses to dress me instead of Peter having to struggle. Quite an improvement over the old days! Many people are very negative about Greek hospital care, but this was excellent. Maybe it was just this hospital, *Agios Savvas*, which was so good.

By Thursday, just two days later, I was allowed to go home.

"Good choice, Barbara!" I thought. Thank God, I had insisted that only the lump be removed.

The ladies who had had the full breast removed were still exercising up and down the corridor, carrying their bags of blood collected from the drain tubes under what had been their breast. I still felt like a woman, not a young boy. I still had a breast and a nipple! I don't think a man could possibly understand how I felt, but for sure a woman would. As far as I was concerned, one breast was better than none. For other women, the peace of mind of having both breasts removed was of more importance. I was grateful that I had been given the choice. Little did I know at this stage, that my treatment was far from over.

I survived the administrative gymnastics of checking out of a Greek hospital, and then, during the following weeks, the challenge of transporting a tumour from one Athens hospital to another for analysis. This was fine for those who lived in Athens, but impossible to do when living on a Greek island. With the help of the hospital volunteers department, I was able to avoid a two-day trip to Athens and they offered to walk the tumour around the corner for me. An appointment was fixed for March with the surgeon who had performed the operation. Unlike many Greek doctors, he was known as one of the few doctors that didn't accept a *'fakelos'*: in this case, an envelope containing a sum of money to ensure that you got the best treatment or, in some cases, got treated at all. It has now been made illegal, but is so ingrained into the Greek culture I still saw ladies slipping money into the pockets of the doctors as they did their rounds. In all our hospital visits neither Peter, nor I, had ever needed to pay a doctor anything, although we knew stories of people that did. I heard of one story where someone paid as much as 3,000 euros just to get treatment, and then the official hospital bill came on top of that because they had no insurance.

The surgeon told me that the tumour was cancerous, but that further treatment would only be a hormone therapy, a pill to take daily. At least I wouldn't need chemotherapy and I rejoiced all the way home. Another appointment was fixed with an oncologist for the following Monday, so another ferry trip and more paperwork hoops to jump through. I was just grateful we had medical insurance through all Peter's years of work and, as his wife, I was covered, too. The oncologist was professional, but extremely brusque, "Of course you have to have chemotherapy: it was cancer!"

The therapy would take 1–2 hours every three weeks and would last six months. Then, I would also need five weeks of radiotherapy. I had to return to Paros, have a cardiologist check that my heart was strong enough for the chemotherapy and then return the following Monday.

Even as I returned a week later, I wasn't in any way convinced I was going to go through with this. I had refused chemotherapy in 1994 and I was still very much alive. Peter said it was time to think big! Ask God to finally restore my breast and if there was no restoration by Monday, then go with the therapy. Someone else felt that chemotherapy was acceptable for an inoperable brain tumour, but not the route for breast cancer when the tumour had been removed. Lornie, God Bless her heart, was amazed that I was even considering chemotherapy.

I phoned Janette, my Christian friend in Canada, who is a top cancer research scientist. What would her advice be, both as a Christian believing in supernatural healing and a professional in the cancer field?

"Well", she said, "If it were me, I'd have the chemotherapy. You see it only takes one cell to have broken off the tumour and to be somewhere in your system and eventually it will show up and attach itself to somewhere in your body. It may take between 5–10 years before you are aware of it, but chemotherapy will blast it out and kill it."

Her comment made me realise what a miracle it was when I was healed sixteen years earlier with no chemotherapy or radiotherapy. Dozing on the sofa the Saturday before my trip, I heard that still, small, inner voice.

"I have provided the best cancer hospital in Europe, given you the insurance, provided a place nearby for you to stay free, just take the chemotherapy and trust me."

In spite of this apparently clear word from God, I still had my doubts. Was that really God speaking or not? As I boarded the ferry to go to Athens, a friend, Harris, and his mother stepped onto the escalator in front of me. Her words helped me a lot. She said,

"Unless God tells you not to do the chemotherapy, you should do it."

That certainly seemed to be a confirmation of what I had heard and there seemed to be wisdom in it. It was also basically what Peter had said: "Do it".

The truth was that it wasn't so much the chemotherapy that I was afraid of, it was the horror of losing my hair. Yes, I could wear a wig but, at the end of the day, I would have to take it off and climb into bed bald. What on earth would I look like to Peter, as a wife with one breast missing, one hacked about and no hair either?! With this in mind, it was with some relief and a complete sense of gratitude that I discovered I could have the "Cold Cap Treatment" which would prevent me from losing my hair. I would have to pay 90 euros a session, but the health system would refund about half of it. Even if I had to pay 50 euros a session and I needed eight sessions, 400 euros would be worth it to me to avoid being bald. What I didn't realise was that it would draw out the agony of the chemotherapy sessions, as it would extend the length of time required at the start and end of each treatment. The cap was something like a padded balaclava helmet. It was kept in the freezer and then placed on my head and fastened under the chin. If you think how much it hurts your hands when you hold a chicken from the freezer, just imagine what that would feel like on your head. It's hard to say whether it was pain I felt or just extreme discomfort and intense cold. I would sometimes shiver so much they would wrap me in a blanket to keep me warm. When the first cap had been on my head for 15 minutes, just as it was warming up a bit and feeling a bit less uncomfortable, they would take it off and replace it with another cold one from the freezer. The concept was that the cold on the surface of the scalp would keep the blood containing the chemicals away from the cold hair follicles on the surface of the skin, so preventing the hair from falling out. Was it really worth the discomfort, not to mention the cost? Yes, for me it was. Talking to the other women, some said the baldness didn't bother them, but not all. One lady said that she was too embarrassed to let her husband see her bald and she never let the children see her without her wig so as not to frighten them.

The chemotherapy itself didn't hurt for the first four sessions and I prayed that I wouldn't feel sick or dizzy. One person I heard of was so dizzy he fell over and broke his hip. Fractures are not uncommon with chemotherapy. Two days after therapy, I wouldn't have much of an appetite and my stomach was somewhat uncomfortable but, during the therapy, I could eat a sandwich and afterwards cheer myself up with an ice cream.

It was on the Sunday after the first chemotherapy that I finally heard God in a way that was unmistakeably Him. I had just listened to a sermon on faith by Bayless Conley, based on Hebrews 11. He preached on Isaiah 52: "He took up our infirmities and carried our diseases". By the time he got to the end, I was sitting there thinking, "So why am I doing chemotherapy? What a faith failure!" Suddenly, God spoke: "You saw the reason with the elder in Yonngi Cho's church who was hospitalised and with Jean Darnall, your Bible college teacher, when she was in hospital. THE SALVATION OF SOULS IS OF MORE IMPORTANCE THAN YOUR COMFORT. I will put people next to you on every ferry trip, in the waiting room at the hospital, the neighbours in the apartment block. Paul's comfort was not My priority: it was preaching to souls in the prisons and on the ship, and through the shipwreck on Malta. My Son's comfort was not the priority; He had to pay the price. Miracles are not the only way I heal – for many, it is a longer, slower path. You are healed, you are not suffering sickness. I am using the treatment process to give you untold opportunities. You are not suffering."

I understood exactly what God was talking about as the elder in Yonngi Cho's church and Jean Darnall were Christians named in books I had read recently. Both of them were people teaching the supernatural healing power of Jesus, yet both of them had ended up in hospital and, through that, God had used them to reach people in the hospital.

And so it was that my routine from March through to May was a trip to Athens every three weeks. When I finally reached the end of May, the end of the first cycle, I was greatly relieved to be told that I would take a break from chemotherapy, do radiotherapy for thirty sessions daily and then resume the chemotherapy with a second cycle of four treatments. Even with the cold cap, my hair had thinned dramatically and I was keen to give it time to recover before another four sessions.

For the radiotherapy I would need to be at the hospital in Athens, Monday to Friday, for six weeks. That was June and July wiped out for spending time on Paros. While everyone else would be coming down to the island to swim and sunbathe, I would be in the notorious summer smog of Athens. It didn't matter; I wouldn't be able to have sun on my head or else my hair could fall out. During the radiotherapy, I couldn't have any sun on my skin either.

Thanks to the kindness of our neighbour, Marouso, I had an apartment in Kypseli to stay in, which was a short bus and trolleybus ride to the hospital. When the famous Athens strikes were in full swing, I would walk both ways to and from the hospital even after therapy. Anna, the friend and neighbour of Marouso, was kindness itself to me. She often brought me a plate of food, knowing that with trips to the hospital I would have little time or enthusiasm for much cooking. The cost of a hotel for six weeks would have been exorbitant, and the shared hostel accommodation offered by the hospital wouldn't compare to having an apartment of my own. I had many opportunities during the day at the hospital to share the gospel and show some love and kindness to some of the seriously ill people I met. Then, in the evening, it was good just to have time alone with God to strengthen me for another day in the jungle of Athens. Fortunately, I was able to return to Peter and Paros each weekend.

The last hurdle, a further four sessions of chemotherapy, finally arrived. This would take me through to the end of October – not a nice prospect, but at least the end was in sight. A wonderful opportunity was to come my way during these final months. South African friends, Heidri and Rowan, had visited us in July. They were booked to go to Israel, a place I had wanted to go to for years. They said that they felt that God wanted me to go with them. That was going to take a miracle! First, it would not have to clash with my chemotherapy schedule. Secondly, Peter had always said it was much too dangerous to go to Israel, and so God would have to move his heart to enable me to go. Thirdly, the cost of the tour, plus accommodation, was almost 2000 euros, a huge amount of money.

As I went up to Athens for my first August appointment with the oncologist, the question was whether he would start the first of the four cycles of chemotherapy that same week. If he did, the Israel trip could slot in between the second and third session, if he didn't, I couldn't go. Joy upon joy, he wanted to start the chemotherapy that Wednesday, so the trip was possible if God would overcome Peter's objections and provide the money. Peter, realizing how much such a trip meant to me and trusting God that I would be well enough to travel, agreed that if I felt up to it, I could go. As for the cost of the trip, we had been given a gift of 1850 euros two years earlier, with instructions to use it for whatever we felt, something personal or something for the church ministry. I had hoped to use it to build a large room upstairs to meet on Sundays, but the passage of time had never confirmed that or provided enough people to need a larger place to meet. We had always had enough to give generously to individual ministries and people in need without the use of the gift, so it was still available. Since the cost of the trip was 1000 for the tour, 350 for the airfare and 500 for the accommodation for ten days, the total was, in fact, exactly 1850 euros. It did seem that God had provided ahead of time for me to go. I had served God and the group on Paros for twenty years without ever taking a salary. In my current, weakened situation, I was ready to be blessed. I felt complete peace about using the gift for the trip.

I had my second session of chemotherapy on the Wednesday, rested at the apartment on Thursday and left on Friday evening for Athens Airport.

"Jerusalem, here I come!"

14 A TRIP TO ISRAEL

The opportunity to escape from the endless routine of hospital appointments and related paperwork was like the prospect of an oasis in a desert to a thirsty man! It was a chance to rest emotionally and to be infused with the peace of God away from the routine of daily life. Like many Christians, I longed to walk where Jesus had walked but, most of all, I longed to see Jerusalem. I wanted to see the walls and the gates, to see the people praying at the Wailing Wall, to walk through the streets and to see how Jewish people live there today. The timing of the trip was perfect as I would be there for Rosh Hashanah, the Jewish New Year. I had extended my stay by two days to be able to experience Yom Kippur, the national day of repentance, prayer and fasting.

I flew into Ben Gurion Airport early on Saturday morning when it was still dark. I was joining people from several other countries including Norway, Germany and, especially South Africa as the family running the tour was South African. A sherut, the name for an Israeli mini bus taxi, had been arranged to collect us from the airport and to drive us to the centre of Jerusalem where we would be

143

staying. We were staying in a house on Yafo Street, a main street right opposite Zion Square, a popular night spot for street performers. It was just fifteen minutes to walk down to the Old City and enter through the Jaffa Gate. The house belonged to Gerrit and Marty and had accommodation for about twenty people. The bedrooms were homely and the bathrooms shared, separate for men and women, reminding me of school trips long ago. Most of our meals were provided, so that saved a lot of trouble and expense searching for restaurants and snack bars.

The tour didn't begin until the Sunday: Saturday being the Sabbath. The whole city was hushed: no cars, except for tourists travelling to and from the airport and shops and restaurants were closed; it was a whole new experience. Heidri and Rowan had planned to visit the home of a Jewish rabbi at lunchtime. Each Sabbath, the rabbi, his wife and family held an open house. Many of the people there would be teenage Jewish boys studying in Jerusalem to learn Hebrew, but there would be others, including some foreigners.

As we walked to their house from where we were staying, we walked three abreast down the middle of the road. There wasn't a car in sight. A few Orthodox Jewish men, some with their families, were on the streets but it was otherwise deserted. Traffic lights went from green to red, but there was nothing to stop. I was fascinated by the different styles of men's dress, all in black but with different styles of strange hats. Some men also had long beards and ringlets at the side of their head.

Outside the rabbi's house, a group of about twenty people were waiting to be invited in. We were greeted warmly and shown to a table slightly to the side of a group of young men. The tables were already laid with grated carrot and beetroot salads. Bowls of water were passed around and each person washed their hands as a normal part of Jewish tradition before eating together. I couldn't help but call to mind passages from the New Testament which included discussions with the Pharisees on the washing of hands. As we ate, different men stood up to share stories or teachings in Hebrew or English. The Hebrew was translated for those of us who didn't understand. There must have been about one hundred or more of us crammed together at the long tables. The rabbi's wife and sons served the food, which had all been prepared the previous day before the start of the Sabbath at sundown on Friday.

The first man to speak told us how many young Israelis were leaving Israel and Judaism; they were going to India. Jewish teachers had been sent to India to win them back to their roots and it was proving very successful. The main reason given by young people for leaving Judaism was to be free from all the restrictions, laws and regulations of the Old Covenant. It really brought home to me how it is so much easier and better to not be under the Law, but rather in our New Covenant with the Lord Jesus.

We sang Shabbat songs from song books containing phonetic Hebrew; the atmosphere was so like singing Greek songs together, but this was worship in Hebrew. Rabbi Mordechai spoke on Deuteronomy 30 and how the Lord will circumcise the hearts of His people so that they will love Him with all their hearts. Much to my surprise, he then invited anyone who would like to speak to do so, particularly encouraging those of us at the visitors table. I had no intention of saying anything; I had wrongly assumed that women wouldn't be allowed to speak. What could I say to a group like this? Anyway, from the time I had arrived, I had felt inexplicably emotional and tears were streaming down my cheeks most of the time.

I was absolutely astonished when Rabbi Mordechai said, "Now, where is that English lady who's here for the first time?"

I felt it would be quite rude to refuse such a gracious invitation, so I sent an arrow-type prayer upwards asking for guidance from the Holy Spirit as to what I could say to such a gathering. I said that I was honoured and blessed to be with them all and that this was my first visit to Israel. I then continued: "There are many places I expect that I will visit during my two weeks here, but a country is not only the land. More importantly, it is the people. For me, just being here with you today is far more special than the places I will visit."

I said that I was English not Jewish, as far as I knew, although my father's name was Reuben. I lived in Greece, not England, because the Lord had called me there. Like Abraham, I had left my home and my family not knowing how I would live in Greece or what I would do there, but that the Lord had been faithful and had guided me and provided for me in that land. I stressed that the Lord was totally faithful and that we could trust Him completely whatever He should call us to do.

There was so much more I could have said about how the Lord guides us, the where, when and how of my call to Greece, but it seemed too much for a first visit and surely others would want to speak. I sat down with my heart pounding and waited to listen to what others would speak about. For now the link had been made. The next time I visited, maybe Heidri and Rowan would not be there to lead me to the house. The route to their home was firmly fixed in my mind. One day, I hoped to return there and tell them more about how faithful our God is.

As it turned out, the next Shabbat we were there again. This time, I was there to listen and not to speak. A young Jewish man told his story of how, when he was a soldier in the Israeli army, he developed a very strange rash which formed lesions on his skin. When he came home on leave, the rash was so bad that he had to go to the hospital and he was not allowed to return to his unit. At 8:05a.m., the exact time he would have returned to his unit, the room where he would have been staying was bombed and several soldiers were killed. Fortunately, his close comrades had been called out on a job and they, too, were spared.

God works in unexpected ways and can even use a sickness to protect or guide someone. It reminded me of the story of an American business man whose car had a flat tyre on his way to the airport in the morning rush hour. By the time he had changed the tyre and made it to the airport, hot and irritated, his plane had left. It was only later in the day that he heard that every person on the flight had died when the plane had crashed. He realised that God had used a flat tyre to save his life. I left the rabbi's house with much to think about.

The first morning of the tour, we started with a trip around the Old City of Jerusalem. It was just a short walk from Gerrit and Marty's house to the Jaffa Gate and then on to the Zion Gate. At the Zion Gate, we noted that the walls were riddled with bullet holes, a reminder of the capture of Jerusalem in 1967 during the Six-Day War.

One of the churches we visited was the Church of the Holy Sepulchre; on our arrival I thought I had been transported back to Greece. It serves as the headquarters of the Greek Orthodox Patriarch of Jerusalem and was overflowing with Greeks. The Anointing Stone commemorates the place where the body of Jesus was prepared for burial – though in reality the stone dates only from 1810; it was surrounded by pilgrims and tourists rubbing cloths and handkerchiefs on it. It was yet another example of people substituting ancient relics for the absence of relationship or the indwelling presence of the Holy Spirit.

Another church we visited was the Dormition Abbey, dedicated to Mary, the mother of Jesus Christ, rather than to Christ. This was supposedly built on the spot where Mary "had fallen asleep", the Christian expression for going to heaven. Greeks never refer to anyone as dying, which makes conversation somewhat difficult for the foreigner to understand. When they say of someone "He's gone", you have to be on the ball to know if they are saying he has gone to Athens or gone to heaven, depending on the circumstances! It is often far from obvious, especially if they are speaking of a very young person.

Gerrit, our group leader, found a quiet corner and began to teach us. We were only twelve in the group which made it much more personal. The basis of all the teaching on the tour was the basic Hebrew roots of the Christian faith.

In order for a person today to understand why Jesus had to die and shed His blood as the one-time sacrifice for our sins, it is necessary to understand the Old Testament animal sacrifices: the blood of the sacrificial animal covered (or atoned for) the person's sin. This animal sacrifice had to be continually repeated. Jesus, however, had to die only once to atone for our sin with His blood. This is why He is called the Sacrificial Lamb.

The very word "sin" is considered outdated by many people who consider they are "good". Jesus, on the contrary, said that no one was good except God. Sin is best understood as an act of disobedience to a divine law. We sin when we know the good we should do and don't do it. We are all sinners in need of forgiveness; it's just that some people have yet to acknowledge it.

As we walked around the church, Gerrit pointed out various symbols and crosses on the mosaic floors and the ceiling which are considered by many uninformed people to be Christian symbols. In reality, many of them are in origin Babylonian from before the time of Christ, and have their roots in the worship of Nimrod, Semiramis and their son Tammuz. Semiramis was worshipped as the "mother of god" and a "fertility goddess". Nimrod is mentioned in the book of Genesis, the first book of the Old Testament, and is surrounded by pagan idolatry, unlike Abraham who worshipped the one true God.

The circle with a cross in it, seen everywhere in the churches we visited, was originally a symbol of Tammuz. The circle represents the sun, relating to the worship of the sun god. Tammuz was conceived in March/April and the feast of Ishtar, or Esther, celebrated fertility. The ancient peoples used the egg and the rabbit as symbols of fertility for obvious reasons. Another horrific practice of the Babylonians was the sacrifice of children to the gods of Molech/Isis and Osiris. They then used the children's blood to dye the eggs red. It was only when I came to live in Greece that I discovered red eggs for Easter and was told that the eggs represent new life and the red is the blood of Jesus. It all sounds very religiously correct but, in reality, the roots of the custom are in Babylonian paganism. So, now, at Easter, we have pagan red eggs and pagan chocolate eggs and rabbits to celebrate what should be the death and resurrection of our Lord Jesus Christ!

The Babylonians also baked buns with raisins, which we have now adapted as hot cross buns for Easter. Of course even the English name Easter comes from the goddess Ishtar. At least the Greeks correctly use the name Pascha, from the Jewish Passover, rather than a word based on a pagan goddess.

Nine months later, at the end of December, the twenty-fifth day was chosen to celebrate the birth of Tammuz. It was their tradition to cut down a tree on the night of 24 December and to decorate it with gold and silver. Tammuz was considered a god and his birthday was always celebrated as a wild, drunken orgy. So there we have the real roots of Christmas trees and why we celebrate Christmas day on 25 December. Shepherds don't usually "watch their flocks by night" in Israel in December: it's too cold! Jesus was most likely born around the time of the Passover, in March or April.

The December festival is also around the time of the winter solstice. Because the days had become shorter and shorter up until 21 December, the sun was thought to be losing its power and the sun had to be reborn, so logs were lit (our Yule log), and lights put on the tree, as they celebrated the lengthening days after 21 December. The tree was kept for seven days when they then lit candles and celebrated the rebirth of the sun on 1 January.

Gerrit then continued to explain how, in 325 AD, the Roman Emperor Constantine wanted to strengthen his empire and sought to do so through religious ideology. He basically looked at the pie chart of the numbers of people in various religious groups in his empire and observed that Christianity formed the largest group. He took Judaism out of the worship and brought in the worship of the sun god on Sunday! He changed the day of worship from the original Jewish Sabbath (sundown Friday to sundown Saturday) to Sunday. In the traditional churches, much of what we now see is Babylonian paganism presented as Christianity. The images now depicting Mary holding the baby Jesus are the same as those which were used to depict Semiramis holding the baby Tammuz. The Queen of Heaven, whom the Jews were worshipping in the book of Jeremiah in the Old Testament, was likely Astarte, or Ishtar. Yes, Jesus was crucified on Jewish Passover and raised from the dead on the third day but, in modern Christianity, it is usually celebrated on a day named Easter after the pagan goddess Ishtar.

This was all news to me and, considering that at this point I had been a Christian for twenty-five years, I wondered how many other Christians, especially Greeks, were aware of this historical background to their religious traditions. This was quite an interesting start to the first day of teaching on the tour.

Monday was to be an exciting day. We were up at the crack of dawn and would drive up to Galilee and stay two nights in a hotel in Tiberius on the Sea of Galilee. As the mini bus began the descent from Jerusalem to the Dead Sea, I had never seen a place so barren in all my life. It wasn't desert sand; it was just miles and miles of bare rock with not a tree or shrub to be seen. Reading the account of Jesus' temptation in the wilderness, I had imagined a barren place but, somehow, with some scrub bush here or there; having had no rain since the spring, there was not a blade of grass to be seen at the end of the summer. Occasionally, we saw groups of Bedouins but no grand tents and carpets, just forlorn shanty towns made of bits of wood and corrugated iron. Pick-up trucks and goats were seemingly more practical than camels, though we did see some camels "parked" outside a place selling clay pots!

As we drew close to the eastern border with Jordan, we swung left onto a main highway to travel due north again. We drove many miles with the Jordan River on our right. Strangely, in the south, on the Israeli side of the Jordan River, the land is barren and virtually uninhabited, yet, on the Jordanian side of the river, we could see lush green fields and many towns. This is simply because Jordan gives Israel no access to the Jordan River water at this point as the river is in Jordan, not in Israel.

As we passed Jericho, now under Palestinian control, we saw the gates, barriers and control points. From where we were on the highway, there was no sign of the ancient city walls as Joshua saw it, just a flat plain and a collection of modern buildings. Reading tourist literature, I understood that one of Jericho's primary sources of income was Christian tourism. A cable car takes Christian pilgrims up the hill to the Mount of Temptation, topped by a Greek Orthodox monastery with panoramic views of the region. The year I saw it, Jericho, with its proximity to the Dead Sea, was declared the most popular destination among Palestinian tourists, but we had no time to visit, we were headed for Galilee.

Here and there, we got our first glimpse of Kibbutzim full of banana groves and vegetables, all now grown on a commercial basis. It was far from the Kibbutz dream of the hippies of the 1960's, working in the Kibbutz for food and a place to live in the sunshine.

Our first stop was Beit She'an National Park, an archaeological site which made even Corinth look insignificant by comparison. Ruled by the Philistines, then

King David of Israel and Judea, the Assyrians, the Greeks, the Romans and then the Arabs, the architecture was a fascinating mixture of styles. Much of it had survived the earthquake of 749AD and considerable restoration work had taken place. The amphitheatre was so magnificent that it could have hosted a modern-day drama with a vast audience. No amplifiers would be necessary as, when Gerrit stood down on the stage and we sat in the seats on the upper rim, we could easily hear him speaking. My word, what fantastic acoustics!

Gerrit pointed out to us that most modern day churches are organised on this Roman concept of the church as a theatre with one or more "actors" up front and the rest of the "audience" seated, watching or learning. By contrast, the Hebrew concept of learning was by discipleship, sharing life together, as Jesus did with his disciples.

Next, we visited Gideon's Cave - Ma'ayan Harod, the Harod Spring Nature Reserve. This was where God selected just 300 of Gideon's 1000 men to fight the Midianites. For us, it was just a sheer delight to sit in the sunshine on the lush green grass next to the spring, listening to a Bible teaching. Of course, I had to retreat into the shade because of my hair follicles and the chemotherapy. I didn't want my hair to fall out, least of all in the middle of the tour.

Then it was on to Megiddo, the plain where the final battle between the people of God and the nations will occur, the Battle of Armageddon. It was amazing to be up on Mount Carmel, with its statue of Elijah in flowing robes, and to reflect on the Biblical prophecies as we looked across to Megiddo.

Finally, we headed towards the Sea of Galilee and our hotel. It had been a long day, but we just had to stop on the way at Yardenit, the baptismal site. It was located where the Jordan River flows from the Sea of Galilee, and was to the south of the city of Tiberias where we would stay. I didn't like it at all: it was so commercialised with gift shops and cafés. Nevertheless, many people chose to be baptised there in Israel and, for those who had never had an adult believer's baptism, it was a good thing to do. For me, I knew that my baptism at age thirty-three, when I came to believe in Christ and received Him as my Saviour, was all that I needed. I had also been baptised as a baby, but it was simply a ritual and I had certainly not received the Holy Spirit at that time. Without faith in Jesus, it had done little for me other than wet my head. It hadn't even been a baptism with full immersion, so it was clearly not a picture of the death, burial and resurrection in Christ.

After checking into our hotel, we went straight down to the shore for a boat trip on the Sea of Galilee before sundown. The old-style wooden fishing boat was large enough to take fifty people, so our group of less than twenty easily boarded. The crew were also musicians and Daniel Carmel was both a fisherman and the worship leader. As we sailed under a gentle breeze, Daniel played keyboards. He sang many of the popular worship songs of the time in both Hebrew and English. To hear "How Great is our God" sung in Hebrew was an experience I would never forget. Now I can sing it regularly with parts in Hebrew, "Gadol Adonai", which means "How great is our God".

It was wonderful to find that I had a room of my own at the hotel. After a Kosher dinner, I opted for an early night. The others could talk all night if they wanted to, but the next day I needed all my strength for the programmed long walks, which would be along rivers and waterfalls. Besides, I needed some time alone with the Jesus whose land I was walking in. I had come to seek Him too, not just His land.

The North of Israel is particularly beautiful to someone who lives on a Greek island which is dry and dusty for six months every year. The Banias falls were a delight to behold, the River Jordan crashing down waterfalls and then flowing through beautiful wooded chasms with dappled sunlight shimmering through the leafy glades. It was a place I would have loved to sit alone for hours with my Bible, enjoying the presence of God, but we had a full schedule. That would have to wait for a visit sometime in the future. The Hula Valley bird sanctuary showed me how pampas grass grows in its natural environment, a lake surrounded by water. No wonder ours in the garden dries up from June to October, even with a bucket of water regularly thrown over it. The migrating birds weren't there in September, but the 3-D film of the birds with sound effects and sprinkled water was almost as good as the real thing. That was something else I wanted to return to see one November, when the birds migrate from northern Europe to Africa.

Another day, we walked atop the rampart walls of Jerusalem, noting the gates, especially the Golden Gate which is firmly locked awaiting the coming of Messiah. We saw the Dome of the Rock, but I was far more interested in the large open area to the north of the Dome, directly in line with the Golden Gate: a most likely spot for the Jewish Temple to be rebuilt, according to Bible prophecy.

Towards the end of the tour, we moved to Masada, the ancient fortification at the south of the Dead Sea situated on top of an isolated rock plateau. This huge flat rock was where the city of refuge was perched high above the flat plain below. I was glad there was a cable car and didn't envy at all the brave souls who had decided to walk the zigzag path to the top.

The days of the tour passed all too quickly. As most of the others in the group left for the airport, I was all set to move to my next hotel near the museum and the Knesset, surrounded by tranquil parks and gardens. Here I would experience Yom Kippur, the national day of fasting. I wanted to rest on my bed with my Bible and focus totally on God, not distracted by food or people. It was like a hush fell over the whole nation: no cars, not many people around, a total calm. What a concept; a whole nation praying at the same time; what power!

Heidri was practising her flute with the orchestra for the ICEJ (International Christian Embassy Jerusalem) celebration on the Feast of Tabernacles in five days' time. Later in the day, when the fast ended after sunset, we would go together to the Synagogue in the centre of Jerusalem. I was so looking forward to seeing what it would be like. Would there be singing? Would there be any images or pictures of Bible stories? Would the women cover their heads? Would the women be in a separate area to the men? I wondered what the prayer would be like and if I would be able to understand. In Jerusalem, I had bought a white, linen dress with a little matching jacket to cover the shoulders. It was most important not to have bare shoulders. I had been told that many wore white to symbolize purity after the repenting and fasting. I was pure and righteous because I had been cleansed in the blood of Jesus. The little white jacket was covered with pretty silver sequins, and it made me feel feminine and pretty after months at hospital not feeling very pretty at all.

I wasn't to be disappointed. The women were in a separate balcony above the men. Many married women covered their heads, but not the younger women. Yes, I could understand the prayer as the prayer book was written in English on the opposite page to the Hebrew. I now have my own Hebrew prayer book and have learnt a lot. The prayer is not without humour though: one prayer by the men is to thank God they were not born a woman!

The singing was magnificent. I had originally thought to stay only an hour and then seek some food after the fast, but the worship was so inspiring I stayed right through to the end. What an experience. This was what Jesus had grown up with, regularly praying at the synagogue.

What an end to my trip. It was time to return to the world of doctors and my seventh chemotherapy. Yet, the end of all that treatment was in sight: just two more chemotherapy sessions to go and by the end of October, it would all be over, thank goodness. A final, perfect set of blood test results arrived in December, and I could move into 2011 knowing that Jesus had rescued me. I was alive, fit, strong and healthy.

We even had a trip to Belgium to look forward to. We had decided to visit Peter's mum and his four sisters. His mum was eighty-six years old, so when she gave up the only bed in the apartment for me and proposed to sleep on the sofa, I protested loudly. It was to no avail; she had determined to bless me after all that I had been through. Peter would sleep on a folding bed at my side and she would be just fine on the sofa. It was fortunately only for a few days.

15 ALL NATIONS

The year 2011 was the year of the curls. My hair, which all my life had been naturally dead straight, grew back curly. I was delighted, and it was good to have thick hair again as it had thinned quite a lot with the chemotherapy. It was also the year of our twentieth wedding anniversary so any photographs would just have to be with curly hair. We decided to make it special by going to Santorini for a few days in early May. We live so close to Santorini, just three hours by ferry, and yet it was probably twenty-five years since I had last visited.

I took more than three hundred photographs in those five days, captivated by the variety of colours of the volcanic rocks. These were mirrored in the chosen colours of every door, wall and window of the cubic houses and the sumptuous hotels clinging to the edge of the cliff. Ochre walls with deep red or green doors were rather unusual on Paros and they provided a refreshing sweep of colour across the vista of Oia, a village to the north of Santorini. In my opinion, the island really had to be the eighth wonder of the world.

On the evening of our wedding anniversary, we had

planned to watch the spectacular sunset over the crater and then eat a wonderful dinner in the Ellis restaurant with its fabulous views. I had chosen it, not just for the interesting menu displayed outside, but also for the linen tablecloths, fine cutlery and beautiful glasses; these were things rather hard to find on Paros. I had hoped to wear a lovely emerald green dress and look feminine for a change, rather than wearing trousers, as is so common with women today. It was not to be; the weather was not the typical, clear blue sky and sunshine of May. Thick, dark, storm clouds were hanging over the island and the crater, blown along by a rather strong wind. The sun was a watery white disc dropping over the horizon, so the expected flaming red sunset over the volcano was not to be. It would have to wait for another trip. Undeterred, we listened to the classical music as the sun set; the meal was as exceptional as I expected and we had a thoroughly lovely evening. I went to sleep that night so thankful for the wonderful husband God had given me and the twenty years we had enjoyed together. There would be many more years yet, I was quite sure of that.

Now that the therapy was over, we could get on with our lives and I could continue with the purpose for which God had called me to Greece. Just a month earlier, Karen from Hellenic Ministries had visited us. She had reminded me of Costas Macris, the founder of Hellenic Ministries, and just how instrumental his arrest had been in my call to Greece. He had given a New Testament to a young boy under eighteen years old and had been sentenced to three-and-a-half years in prison! I knew that God had brought me to Greece for a purpose and I suspected it was more than had happened to date. Living on an island with such a steady stream of tourists always provided plenty of opportunities for one to one evangelism as, with so many people into New Age philosophy, many have no idea why they need Jesus.

Back home on Logaras beach, I was conscious of what

a great place it was for family holidays. Santorini wasn't really a place for beautiful beaches, whereas at Logaras there were several really good beachside restaurants and trees for shade in the midday blistering heat. For many years, we had regularly eaten at the Fisilani's restaurant since we knew the family so well. We had also become friendly with one of the Albanian waiters. He was incredibly popular with many of the customers and had a gift for languages that made it easy for him communicate in Greek, English, French, German, Italian, and a bit of Swedish. The list was seemingly endless. Apparently, having girlfriends from a variety of different nations was a great language school! When we heard that he had finally settled down, was married and had a daughter, we were delighted. So, it came as a bit of a shock to hear that his wife, Dorina, had broken her leg in a bike accident. The break was particularly serious and they had taken her to an Athens hospital, where a metal plate was inserted in her upper thigh to hold the two pieces of bone in place. On visiting her, I found her to be a pretty vivacious young girl, with long, flowing dark hair, a winning smile, and very easy to talk to. Much to my amazement, I discovered that she spoke rather good English, too. It transpired that as a young girl living in Albania she had received Christ and been baptised. Some American missionaries had started a church in a town near her village and both she and her brother Eri had been baptised. I asked her if she would like me to pray for her leg to be healed, and she was very pleased to accept the offer. At that time, she was on crutches and, when she started to walk without the crutches, she limped quite badly and still had a lot of pain. On a later visit to the hospital to have the bone checked, the doctor was amazed that she was walking at all. He told her that many people with a break in the place she had, ended up in wheelchairs, so she was doing really well. Prayer really does work.

Over the months that followed, I regularly visited the

family and, though they rarely came to join us on Sundays, Dorina was able to join us for some of our midweek prayer meetings. From her early church days, she knew many of the worship songs we used, and we had high hopes for her and all the family. When, on a Sunday in December, Dorina and her daughter joined us with her sister and her mother, I hoped that we had an Albanian revival in the making. For a long time they didn't come again. Then finally, Alex did arrive one Sunday at the end of 2012 and received Christ and took communion with us. He was so excited that he told all his family that he had received Christ. Naturally, we encouraged him to follow through with baptism.

It was some time later that I discovered that Dorina was using Facebook to keep in touch with Dana and Larry Stucky, the American missionaries that had been involved with establishing the church in Korca, Albania. Dorina and her brother Eri had been a part of the worship group in the nearby village of Sheqeras. Dana and Larry had returned to live in America in 2011, after eighteen years in Albania, but their daughter, her husband and two children were still serving the Lord in Albania. It seemed that Dorina and Alex had invited Dana and Larry to visit Paros when they next travelled to Albania from the States. I felt that I should contact them to make an initial introduction and to ask if they, or anyone else from the Albanian group, might be interested to come and help us to disciple these precious Albanians. It was all well and good teaching Dorina and her sister in English but, for their mum and dad with their limited Greek, it was obvious that Albanian would be better.

I was delighted to receive a reply saying that not only were they willing to come, but that it might be possible to bring two or four people from the Korca church to help with evangelism and preaching. The question was, in June, how available would the Albanians be for visits or meetings? And that was a big question. It was normal in the summer for the men to work two jobs: building or painting by day and working as waiters by night. The women cleaned all day and then in the evenings needed some time to prepare food and do things at home. Nevertheless, we went ahead and prepared an outline program for a five-day visit and started to learn the names of the Albanian pastor and his wife and son, ready for the visit.

Imagine our shock when we received an email the day that Dana and Larry should have been flying to Albania, telling us that Dana was in the operating theatre in America and they had missed the plane and lost their tickets. After that, it seemed that our link had been lost for this visit and it would be difficult to go ahead without them. I was most discouraged. It just seemed that all of the outreaches we had tried on the island were either unfruitful or called off before they happened. Were we not hearing God re His strategy for Paros, or was there some spiritual stronghold that we needed to break first? It would take a few years longer before we would begin to understand this.

God had promised me that He would use the treatment Loula process of the breast cancer to provide me with untold opportunities for the salvation of souls. It was on another return trip from Athens for a check-up that I met three very interesting, yet unusual Greek people on the ferry coming home. They were actually living in Canada and so visited Greece from time to time. I opened up a conversation with the two elderly Greek ladies who turned out to be very strong Christians. Voula was a mature woman of God who knew Johnathan Macris of Hellenic Ministries, and she even had the same New Testament with her that we had distributed in the early days. She was leading Bible studies in the Greek Orthodox church in her home town in Canada. It seems the Orthodox Church in Canada was quite happy for older women to teach other women and the children. We prayed together for her sister, her brother, and for the nation of Israel. Her sister was also a woman of God and so we agreed to meet up on Paros for our next prayer meeting.

Voula also sent me her written testimony, a very moving story of love, betrayal and forgiveness which we decided to relate here. We hope that through sharing her personal, painful experience it will help other people suffering in similar situations to find the answer they are searching for. Here follows her touching story, including how it affected her father:

"My name is Voula and I was born in Vryna, Krestena, Greece. I finished High School in Krestena, and succeeded in my exams for entry into post-secondary education to become a high school educator through the Arsakio Academy in Patras. However, in 1958, I made the decision to emigrate from my homeland and move to the beautiful city of Vancouver, on the very west coast of Canada.

Shortly afterwards, I brought my soon-to-be husband from Greece, and we were married in January 1962. God gave us two beautiful children, a daughter in 1964, and a son in 1966, even though the doctors said we wouldn't be able to have children because of my condition with endometriosis. But the greater physician from above answered my prayers.

In 1974, we moved from Vancouver to another beautiful waterfront city. There we bought a property and opened a service station and gas bar as my husband was not only an automobile mechanic, but he was also considered a specialist in his trade and worked with foreign cars.

Life was beautiful. We worked hard, but it was also very rewarding. We both loved people and we were both givers. In fact, many times he would not charge people for the work he did on their cars if he realized they were struggling financially. But God always gave back to us in His own way. The Bible says: 'Give and it shall be given unto you'.

On that same property we built a 24-unit motel. Our

daughter had just graduated with a Bachelors degree in Psychology from the University of British Columbia. She became the manager in the motel and coordinated the day-to-day operations, furnishings, systems, the hiring, and running of the business. Vancouver was hosting the world exposition 1986 and the motel was built to capitalize on the multitude of visitors coming to see the Exposition.

One of the cleaning ladies hired was of Indian origin and married with two children. She was having issues with her husband. She would often spend time talking about how he regularly treated her badly. One day, my husband came to me and said, 'Voula, we should help this woman'. So I met with her, talked to her and tried to comfort her. I encouraged her to seek professional help and try to save her marriage. I bought her a Bible in her native Sikh language and even took her to a Christian women's retreat for support.

My husband had accepted the Lord into his heart and we had both been baptised in the Jordan River in the Holy Land. Even so, it was not long before he left me for her! She wounded me greatly! I could not believe it! I truly thought my life was OVER! It had never come to my mind that this would EVER happen to me. I thought we were so secure.

I soon fell into a deep depression. I did not eat or drink and I kept the excruciating pain to myself. My children saw my pain and they suffered along with me. My daughter said, 'Mum, you need to see a counsellor, you cannot go on like this.' I said, 'Not yet, not yet'. One day, in frustration she said, 'If you do not make an appointment yourself, I will make one for you and drag you there.'

One day, I was alone at home. I got a cup of coffee and went to our family room downstairs and turned on the TV. There was a Christian program showing and it was almost at the end. I heard the woman who was speaking say, 'Is there anyone here who would like to ask God anything? Just ask Him.' I thought to myself, 'Do I ever have something to ask Him? He's the only one that knows what I am going through.' Right there I knelt down and said, 'Jesus, you are the only one that knows what I am going through. Please help me. Thank you. I believe you will help me through this.' I was at the end of my rope. Tears were running down my face like a river. I felt my body was a pile of flesh with no bones or muscle. I don't know how long I knelt there, but when I returned upstairs I was a different person. A beautiful peace had come upon me. I looked outside and all of a sudden everything was more beautiful. The trees, the flowers, the birds and their song, all came to life. There was a beautiful, sweet peace in my heart. I didn't know what was happening to me. The only thing I knew was that I had asked Jesus to help me, and He had.

I opened the Bible and God led me to John 3:3, the story of Jesus and Nicodemus, where Jesus answered to Nicodemus: 'You must be born again to enter the kingdom of God'. We have been born into this world and in the flesh from our parents, but later we need to be born from the Holy Spirit and invite Him into our hearts. Even though I had been teaching in Sunday school from a young age, I didn't really know Jesus. In our church we were taught the right way, but we did not focus on the relationship between us and Jesus, nor His promises. His promises include: 'I will always be with you, I am holding you by the right hand, and when your time comes to leave this place, you will be with me in my glory'. What a beautiful promise and such assurance Jesus gives us.

When Jesus changed my life, I wanted everyone around me to have what I found, especially my parents because they were old. They were good people, church-goers and believers. They needed what Jesus said to Nicodemus to be spiritually born again. So I tried to explain to my father but it was hard for him to understand. He said, "I taught religion to you and now you want to teach me?!" 'Father, I said, 'our religion is good, but I am talking to you about

Jesus; we need Him in our lives'. 'We need the Holy Spirit, to invite Him into our hearts, and our names to be written in the Book of Life.'

Good works alone will not save us. When Jesus is in our hearts, we have love, because God is love, and with His love in our hearts we will do the good works and love one another. It's God's love in us and not just our love that will help us to help others.

After our parents left to go to Greece, I felt really bad because my parents had not come to know the Lord personally. But God had a plan and He gives us the desires of our hearts. Praise His holy name! My father got sick in Greece and the three of us, my brother, my youngest sister and I, ran to be with him in Greece. He had a hernia and, according to the doctors, it would be dangerous for him to have an operation because it was feared he might not wake up from the anaesthetic. After being with him for many weeks, we were down to one week before leaving for Canada again. I went to Patras to see my aunt, my father's sister, and the next day we travelled by bus back to my father. While I was on the bus, I heard a voice saying, 'Take your father to the doctor'. I told my father that, since we were leaving for Canada again shortly, it would be a good idea to see the local doctor and get another opinion.

After some time and a few examinations, the doctor said emphatically, 'This man needs surgery immediately'. He was booked for surgery the next day. I said to my father, 'Tomorrow, you are going for surgery so, as you are old, would you like to pray to ask Jesus to come into your heart?' Do you know what he said? 'Yes my dear'. We quickly went to the small bedroom next to the kitchen, and I asked my father to repeat the words I would say as a Sinners Prayer:

1. Father, I am a sinner, please forgive me.

2. Jesus, I believe in You; You shed your blood on the cross and washed me of all my sins.

3. By faith I invite You to come into my heart.
4. Thank you, Amen.

When I stopped, my father continued by saying the Lord's Prayer loudly and enthusiastically. Praise His holy name. The next day, he had the operation and everything was okay. Next to my father's bed was another man who had had the same operation; he was younger than my father, but nothing was going right with him. He was angry, upset and swearing. I said, 'Jesus, I cannot thank you enough for seeing my father with God's peace in his heart'. Nothing is better than the peace and love we feel when God is living in our hearts. If we have everything but we don't have God in our hearts, we have nothing. All the things in the world cannot fill the empty hole in our heart, neither riches, nor money, nor drugs, nor women, nor men. These things give us pleasure for a short time, but God's love is forever.

We can't thank Jesus enough for what He did for us. Adam was cast out of Eden because of his rebellion and because of sin. Jesus, the second 'Adam', opened again the door of paradise for you and for me to enter. And where is the key? The key is in your heart. That is faith in God.

Later on, my husband got cancer. He agreed to have the priest come to his home for a blessing and communion. I showed the priest to the door and then, as I was collecting my things to leave, I heard a voice saying, 'Pray, pray, pray'.

I asked my ex-husband and his partner if they would like to hold hands and pray together. They agreed to do this. I led the prayer and said, 'We have all done wrong things and need to ask God for forgiveness'. While we were praying and crying, I felt water like a river running down my shoulder. On my right-hand side, his partner had leaned her head on my shoulder and could not stop crying. God forgave each one of us and that river of tears opened the door for love and peace to come into our hearts. We turned and hugged and kissed each other in His love. What a beautiful moment in God's presence. What peace; what cleansing; what tears; only He can do this! Thank you, Jesus."

As I finished reading Voula's testimony, there were tears in my eyes. They were tears of sadness because of the pain she had suffered and tears of joy that she had seen those she loved most safely on the path to salvation. What a privilege to have met such a lovely lady and to have been able to hear this wonderful story of forgiveness.

Another story of God leading me to those he wanted me to talk to was a man I met on a ferry travelling to Paros to meet his girlfriend. She ran a hotel in the main town and he also wanted to show the island to his family. He was wonderfully Greek, very handsome, smartly dressed and absolutely charming. From the conversation it became apparent that he was also quite wealthy. It was therefore not surprising he commented that, like a lot of men in his position, he had many temptations to overcome!

I found him very easy to talk to and God opened up a door right there and then. He started to ask many questions, like,

"Why did Jesus have to die?"

"Why did Abraham have to almost sacrifice his son?"

"Why did Job lose almost everything?"

He knew quite a few of the Bible stories, and it was really quite wonderful to answer his questions. In the Greek New Testament, together we read Matthew 24 about the end time return of Christ. Then we looked at Revelation 21 about the destiny of the believers and the unbelievers using Galatians 5 as a barometer to test an individual's spiritual position. It was then time to use the prayer included in chapter two of my original book, *To Greece and the Islands*. As he read out loud the prayer of repentance, tears filled his eyes. Now, he needed God's Help to remain strong, to walk the walk and to overcome the temptations.

This man who Barbara speaks is my brother Nick

Generally speaking, I was talking to all these people not only because of their need of salvation, but also because I really cared about the situations they were struggling with: health issues, financial issues and marital problems. In Greece, when greeting one another, people will often say, "Health above all", meaning it is the most important thing in life, without which you can't enjoy life. In latter years I had learnt not to agree but to reply, "salvation above all, health second". It was a way of opening up a conversation, particularly with Greek people, and at the same time declaring an important truth. It would be debatable that health was really the most important if a person lived all their life in perfect health and then died and spent eternity in hell. Life is relatively short compared with the forever of eternity.

At this point, I was unaware just how many people that I knew really well were about to be diagnosed with different kinds of cancer. It was like an epidemic had just struck. I genuinely believed the name of Jesus was the key to their healing and all that I had to do was to explain it to them. What I had just been through was the training ground to understand their suffering, especially the chemotherapy which I had tried so hard to avoid.

Such was the situation with some retired English friends who came to Paros regularly, once or twice a year. The husband of one couple had been diagnosed with cancer. For years, we had enjoyed their company, while sitting at our local *kafenion* at the back of Logaras beach as the sun set. He and his wife had many an interesting story to tell. Once, at a dinner party with several other friends, I had asked him what he thought happened to people when they die. He said he supposed it was just like the lights being turned out, the end, nothing really. Now I suppose it is possible that a person could have actually received Jesus as their Saviour, yet have been taught nothing about what happens when we die. However, I really thought that everyone who had received forgiveness and had the Holy

Spirit living in them would have understood that they would go to heaven to be with Jesus when they died. The Bible tells us: "grace might reign through righteousness to bring eternal life through Jesus Christ our Lord", and "Jesus Christ, the hope of glory". Isn't that what the gospel is all about? The conversation was definitely an indicator that I might need to talk to him further, but probably not at a dinner party.

Again and again, sitting at the *kafenion*, the opportunity had never really presented itself, so, because I cared so much, I felt that I would write him a letter. I tentatively suggested that, like all of us, he too might need to put matters right with God and to repent. With the letter, I enclosed the Gospel of Luke and the Gospel of John. David Watson's book, *Is Anyone There?*, had been effective in the past, so I gave him a copy of that to read. I also mentioned that Jesus is coming back soon to take the believers up to heaven and that we all need to be quite sure that we are ready to be caught up with Him in the clouds.

My friend eventually died. If, before reading my letter, he was secure with Christ, then it was still a good preparation for his departure to glory. In the event that he was not safely in the kingdom of God, then it had given him another chance to hear the free offer of Christ and to receive salvation. I had just done my part, doing what all Christians should be doing for their sick friends.

What I didn't know at the time was that three others in that group of eight friends would also die within a very short space of time. I had sent the letter to one man who maybe could benefit from hearing the gospel afresh, yet God knew in advance what was about to happen and the letter had been read and discussed by eight people. It gave each one of them another chance if they needed it.

Nevertheless, each one of those with cancer that I had prayed for had eventually died. I was puzzled. What was the missing key?

I was consoled by the fact that some people were

receiving Christ before they died. Such was the case with a Greek family of four, when the husband and father of the family became sick with lung cancer. Because I knew his eldest daughter well from helping her with her Cambridge Proficiency English exam preparation, I was able to visit them and to teach them about the healing power of Jesus through God's written and spoken word. Several times we would gather around the kitchen table and read verses from the New Testament together. Since the extended family was very large, often there would be others visiting while I was there, so they got to hear my stories of Jesus healing others I'd prayed with, and realised that they too needed to repent.

Some weeks after we began to pray, we received the news that the tumour had shrunk from 8cm to 2.3cm and we were all ecstatic with joy. We thought it would not be long before the tumour completely disappeared. The most special days of all were when we sat around the kitchen table together and prayed a prayer of repentance to receive Christ as Saviour. Quite early on when I was together with the two daughters, I had led them to pray a prayer of repentance. The elder sister had read my book so she understood well enough the concept of needing to be born of the Holy Spirit, at some point in her life, by receiving Christ as Saviour. Then, shortly, after the news of the tumour shrinking, I was also able to sit with her father and mother and lead them in a prayer of repentance and salvation.

Yet somehow, in all these months, I was having difficulty helping them to understand that we must keep our eyes on Jesus and pray to the Father, Son and Holy Spirit alone. It is Jesus who died on the cross for our salvation and healing, not the Virgin Mary, (or the *Panagia* as she is called in Greece), nor the saints, including the saints after whom they were named. If a person is praying for healing to Jesus, the Virgin Mary and their saint, then who is going to get the glory for the healing? God made it plain enough in the book of Isaiah, "I will not give my glory to another, or my praise to idols" It is Jesus, and Jesus alone, that heals us and receives the glory. He doesn't need any help from His mum! He is God!

This very special man finally died. I was so peaceful that he had received Christ before he died and that he had forgiven those who had hurt him during his life. He had gone in peace. I was grateful for the part I had been able to play, but he was a great loss to me and all his family.

As the summer came to an end, it was time to remember that my life wasn't only praying with people. There had to be some times to rest and enjoy some of the perks of living on a Greek island. One of them was being able to visit other Greek islands relatively cheaply and easily. The years of not being able to afford a holiday were over as Peter had his pension now. A trip at the end of the summer was most attractive as an opportunity to get away from everyone and all our responsibilities, a chance to enjoy some quality time, just the two of us. Going for a romantic dinner for two was almost impossible throughout the whole summer as there were just so many people around that we knew and who wanted to go out to eat together.

So it came about that we started to try to visit another island each year, at the end of September and early October, before the weather broke and the winter rains started. My idea of a holiday is plenty of resting time lying horizontally with a good book, soaking up some gentle sunshine. Some sightseeing and touring the island is fine, but preferably two or three hours at a time, not an all-day trek.

For years I had wanted to go to Amorgos. Even the name conjured up love and romance and I had heard that Amorgos now is what Paros used to be twenty-five years ago. We found a wonderful room right in the harbour, so we would be close to the restaurants for our evening meal and not have a long climb back to our room at bed time.

We had two balconies, one very large and a perfect place to enjoy breakfast. The curtains and bedspreads all matched in a most stunning turquoise that captured the colour of the sea. Amorgos must have the most brilliant blue waters of the whole Aegean, especially the area under the famous Hozoviotissa monastery.

The monastery hangs precariously to the side of a cliff, neither at the top nor bottom, and how they ever built it is a challenge to the imagination. The cliff is so steep it's hard to conceive how, before the steps were built, donkeys could carry stones and wooden beams. Even today, they have a system of pulleys and a basket to bring up the groceries; maybe that provides a clue. A visit requires strong legs and a good heart as to get there we had to climb some 300 or more steps. The priests are most welcoming to those who make the effort. The whole building is only five metres wide and, after climbing more steps through narrow, stone-walled corridors, we were welcomed into their lounge area. The walls are adorned not only with the most splendid paintings of previous priests, but also heroes of the past, soldiers or commanders who protected the island and the monastery from pirates. We were served delicious *loukoumia*, or Turkish Delight as we call it in English, but in Greece it would be insensitive to refer to it as Turkish anything. Even at eleven o'clock in the morning, small glasses of *rakomeli* were served as part of the hospitality. It's a raki made from fermented grape skins mixed with local honey, for which Amorgos is famous.

We learnt later that the building comprises eight floors and nearly one hundred rooms, although on our visit it appeared to be much fewer. In former times there were far more people who wanted to live a life of seclusion and celibacy. At the time of our visit, there were only three priests living there full time, one of whom had been there for more than forty years. There are obviously monk's cells where they slept, as well as dining halls, ovens and storage areas, but we didn't see them on our visit. They had even established a small garden for vegetables on a rocky ledge and their rainwater is collected in wells, as it would be difficult to carry it up or down by donkey.

Our visit over, we emerged into the dazzling sunlight and heat, a striking contrast to the cool of the stone-walled monastery. I was amazed at how many caper bushes were clinging to the rocks, having tried unsuccessfully for years to get a caper bush established in our garden. Evidently, nature is so much better at these things! As we descended the path, a swim in the sparkling blue waters of the bay below seemed like a good idea before we headed into the village in search of lunch, or at least an iced coffee.

In contrast to trips like Amorgos, in 2013, we decided to see what life as a pensioner on Paros was really like. In the nearby village of Marpissa was a pensioners' club called "*KAPI*" in Greek. They had regular outings twice a year, usually May and October, when they would go on a trip further afield than we could manage just using the local ferries. A trip had been arranged to Thessaloniki and Alexandropolis, both up in the north of Greece, on the east coast. We would need a coach to take us, and everything was arranged for the trip. Since we were able to travel out of season, the group had booked four and five star hotels at fantastically reduced prices. We were able to enjoy the ferry, all coach transport, and four night's accommodation with breakfast for less than 200 euros. We were in for a treat. We had heard that the locals really had fun on these trips and, my word, they did! After the four and a half-hour ferry trip, the coach had barely pulled out of Piraeus when the first box of biscuits was passed around. During the six-hour journey we enjoyed a continual round of biscuits and cheese pies and listened to their songs, their jokes and their stories. How generous they all were! When they started dancing up and down the aisle of the bus, we knew we were experiencing a truly authentic Greek outing! We were the only two non-Greeks on the bus, so it was just as well we spoke and understood Greek quite well. In just five days we visited so many places. We saw the place where Lydia, the first Christian in Greece, had been baptised when Saint Paul came over to Greece from what is now modern-day Turkey. Arriving back at the bus, we discovered that we were the last to board and cries of "The foreigners are missing!" had preceded our entrance!

The nearby ancient city of Philippi was an amazing place; a whole city of archaeological ruins so large that I could have happily spent the day there. We also had a silk factory to visit, learning how they bred the silkworms and harvested the crop. My gift from Peter on that visit was a beautiful green and blue silk scarf. Then, later that day, we visited a national park in the wooded hillsides, where we could go to observation points and watch the eagles nesting. The film we watched of the eagles was inspiring, nature at its best.

It wasn't only trips that we enjoyed as members of the pensioners' club. I had keep-fit/gymnastics twice a week, using light weights so that our arms wouldn't go all wrinkly, as well as bending and stretching on our sponge mats on the floor. For the other ladies it was just a keep-fit class, for me it was that and a Greek lesson.

There were several lunches together throughout the year and the Christmas meal in Aliki, which, at only five euros, was as good as any wedding banquet. It included live bouzouki music, dancing and, on one occasion, a group of people singing traditional island songs. Since joining the ladies keep fit class and going on the trips, we were no longer foreigners sitting on the perimeter, but part of the village community. That was very precious to us.

Before the year of 2013 ended, I was grateful to God that the life of my friend, Maria, had been spared in a terrible car accident near to where we lived. A young Australian man had been riding a quad bike and he was badly hurt and ended up in a coma. Maria was fraught with worry to think that she had been a part of the accident, even though witnesses said that she was on her own side of the road when the young man had pulled out in front of her. He was with his fiancée, who had fortunately been on a separate bike, and a group of friends from Australia. How we prayed for the life of that young man, Luke. For weeks he was in a coma, his strong, muscular body withering away as he was drip fed day by day. At one of our Thursday prayer meetings, I felt strongly that I should command him to wake up in Jesus' name and, glory to God, he did on that very day. We received the news from Maria, who was in contact with the family.

It just so happened that I had another of my hospital check-ups at the time he was in hospital in Athens. After much prayer, I felt that I should visit him and, fortunately, the hospital he was in was not far from where I had my check-ups. On arrival at the hospital, I was relieved to find that I was allowed to visit and entered his room to meet him, his fiancée and also his mother, who had flown in from Australia. I explained that I was a friend of Maria's, the lady driving the car, and that we had been praying for Luke. I also said that I wanted to be sure that Luke had had the opportunity to receive Christ if he were not already a believer. They assured me that they were believers and attended church regularly, so they were more than happy for me to lay hands on Luke and pray for his complete healing. He had broken his leg and walking was out of the question for the moment. I prayed with him and blessed him and his fiancée and his mother. Months later, Maria showed me photos on Facebook of his home and the place where he worked, and that he was finally able to go back to work. As the family appealed for money via Facebook to cover his medical expenses and their loss of wages, I wondered if any of them had thought to help out Maria. Her car was a write-off and, on Greek wages, it would be challenging to get the money together to buy a replacement. As I looked at the photos of the fabulous house they had bought in Australia and compared it to the modest apartment Maria rented for herself and her children, I felt it was a pity that none of the financial help raised ever came her way. I decided it was better not to ask them. We did what we could to help and left the rest to prayer and God. Finally, she did receive some money from the insurance company of the quad bike. God is so faithful.

As if this wasn't enough for anyone to go through in one year, it was only a short time later that Maria's brother suffered a heart attack, a stroke and a ruptured aorta. It was a miracle that he didn't die immediately, but God in His grace and mercy chose for him to live. When he finally arrived back home on the island, he had lost his memory and to this day he doesn't recognise his wife. He knows his sister, brother and his mother, but his wife, who entered his life more recently, has been lost to his memory. He has also not been able to work since the heart attack.

It might seem to be a terrible tragedy and of course it is, but how God has worked for the good in this may help all of us to understand why, sometimes, God doesn't stop these awful things from happening.

Giorgos, like most male Polish workers on the island, was working in the construction industry. He and the others in his team worked hard all day and enjoyed having a few beers at the end of a day's work. The Polish are also known for their love of vodka. As pork was one of the cheapest and tastiest meats to grill, they would often sit and grill sausages and pork chops for their evening meal. It was all good fun, but not a wise or a healthy diet, rather a silent disaster just waiting to happen. All that fat and alcohol on a regular basis was just asking for trouble. Now, while many Polish Catholics grow up in the Catholic Church, rather like the Greeks do in the Greek Orthodox Church, just going to church on the main festivals doesn't actually make a person a Christian. Only God knows what Giorgos' destiny would have been if he had died that day.

As a result, I was able to go to the house and visit him several times. Even on my first visit, I was able to share enough stories of healings and explain their need to repent and to receive forgiveness. It was a wonderful evening to sit outdoors and pray with Giorgos, his wife Paula, and Maria and her mum. I am confident that when Giorgos' life is over on this planet, if he continues in his faith, he will be welcomed with open arms by Jesus His Lord and Saviour. That may not have been the situation prior to his heart attack. People on the prayer chain around the world continue to pray for the restoration of Giorgos' memory, even though doctors say that medically, it becomes more unlikely with the passage of time.

So again, what is better? To live a carefree life without tragedies or health problems and then be eternally separated from Christ, never having received Christ as Saviour, or to suffer in some way that opens our eyes to a God who loves us and to cry out to him for salvation and healing? I suppose we would all prefer to skip the suffering and receive Christ while all is well in our life, but how many people actually do that?

That question was equally applicable to an English man living on the island. His was a spectacular healing which must be included to demonstrate the greatness of God even to those who are supremely disinterested in God or His help. The man had been living on the island for several years, but I had never really met him since he kept himself to himself. When disaster struck I had no access to him to help him directly.

I learnt that he had had some indigestion problems and had been taking medication which was very strong and definitely not to be taken on an empty stomach. One day, in this same year as Maria's trials, his stomach burst and he was rushed to hospital in Athens, where he spent several months in intensive care. He was operated on four times. I became aware of his situation through a friend, who, understandably, asked us to pray for him. We did pray regularly and with confidence even though I was told he was a declared atheist. The idea of him dying in that condition was unthinkable. Week by week, we held him up in prayer, interceding for his very life. When I visited him in hospital, I learnt from his sister that the doctors had said he had only a five percent chance of survival. Only after he had pulled through did we discover that, in the last seven years, his was the first case of this kind where the patient had actually survived. Thanks to a link with his sister and his cousin, who visited him throughout the crisis, I was able to give them each a copy of my first book, and I continue to pray that one day they will each receive Christ. The choice is theirs, but at least he now has a second chance. Without prayer and the grace of God, it would have been too late.

16 A VISIT TO FFALD-Y-BRENIN

There was something about the year 2014 that marked a distinct change in the spiritual atmosphere on Paros. For about five years, three of us had been praying every Thursday for people and situations on the island, as well as for the nation of Greece. Sometimes, we were joined by Christian visitors to the island; sometimes, by those living on the island, but finding it hard to come regularly due to work commitments. Nevertheless, we three foreign women formed the core prayer team and were grateful for any extra support available. By this time I'd been on Paros twenty-five years, Swiss Annamarie twenty years and Jenny from New Zealand longer than us all, an amazing thirty-seven years. She had come in her youth, fallen in love with a handsome Greek, married and now had two grown-up sons living back in New Zealand.

Towards the end of 2013, I felt that three people just weren't enough to get the job done on Paros; we needed to call in some help. Since Christians who knew how to pray were in short supply on Paros, this had to be outside help. So it came about that, around November 2013, we started a world-wide prayer chain of Christians who had visited Paros or lived here for a time. The results of this were nothing short of miraculous!

It was also about this time that I became particularly aware of the spiritual battle that goes on over geographical areas to try to hinder prayer and all efforts at evangelism. There were places in the world, such as Argentina, where, for years, evangelistic efforts bore little or no fruit, until a team of prayer warriors started to intercede and storm the area with prayer.

It was as I read two books by Peter Wagner, *Spiritual Warfare* and *The Queen of Heaven,* that I began to understand what was going on over Paros. I also began to understand the potential dangers of what we were doing. It was in light of this that I was particularly interested in a book called *High Level Warfare Safe from Counter attack.* Having battled cancer twice, anything that could just help to keep me and the others alive was worth investigating. It was while reading this book, I became aware that the author had links with Greece, as she made a comment about being particularly interested in Greece.

I decided to Google search on "Ana Mendez Ferrell and Greece" and was surprised to discover the name of a ministry in Athens that, in twenty years, I had never even heard mention of. It was the Shalom Prayer Centre Athens. On further investigation, it seemed that this was finally a ministry of like-minded Christians. It was led by a Greek couple, George and Evi Markakis, and it seemed appropriate that we should at least get together. Since I had to go up to Athens in early March for my annual mammogram, we arranged that we should meet up later the same day. They very kindly invited me to stay overnight at their house out near the airport and, since their nearest station was on the same metro line as the hospital, it couldn't have been easier.

The hospital appointment completed, I arrived at their house around two o' clock, the time most Greek people eat lunch. Evi's mum had cooked a terrific *Spanakopita* (spinach pie) and there was roast chicken as well. We were five people, including a visiting young German man, Emmanuel, who was staying with them for several weeks. After lunch, George gave me his undivided attention, answering many of the questions that I'd been storing up for the last ten years with no one on Paros to ask. We talked particularly about everyone in the church being a Royal Priesthood and I asked much about spiritual warfare. After several hours teaching, we jumped in the car, together with his wife and Emmanuel, to drive to the prayer centre in Athens for the Monday evening meeting. During the course of the journey, Emmanuel asked me what kind of ministry I had.

"Oh, I don't really feel I have a ministry as such", I replied. "I share my testimony with tourists I meet on the beach or in cafés and use books to help preach the gospel to them. We have a small house church in our home, which provides a meeting place to disciple non-Greek speaking residents and visitors. It's all a bit disappointing really; I sometimes say I am suffering from divine discontent." At such a response, George, who was driving at the time, quite rightly hit the roof and rebuked me severely. "Don't you ever call anything God is doing small or insignificant, belittling His work."

I said that I was only exercising humility, not to boast in any way, but he replied that it was a false humility and totally inappropriate. In response, I told them of the many people God had led to us to be baptised, particularly the South African couple who found me through my first book *To Greece and the Islands,* the Swiss man teaching the youth groups, and the American young man in the art school choir ensemble on Paros. George was right, many people had received Christ and then settled in churches where they lived, and some had been healed as well. My negative outlook came from years of often being only four to six people at a Sunday meeting and the regular criticism from those in other churches who didn't adequately understand the role of women in ministry; we can read about their roles in the early church. Regular comments like, "As a woman, I shouldn't baptise people" or "as a woman, I shouldn't serve the Communion" had somewhat ground me down. The burning flame I'd been when I first came to Greece had dimmed somewhat. A teaching later in the year would finally knock all that on the head and bring a correct Biblical interpretation of the controversial passages on women in the New Testament books of Corinthians and Timothy.

The meeting that night wasn't a bit what I was expecting. I expected to be praying for hours and interceding for the nation of Greece, which is actually quite hard work. Instead, we entered into a totally refreshing time of beautiful worship led by Emmanuel playing keyboards, starting with "How Great is our God". There then followed a time of prophetic ministry with George, Evi and the team prophesying over different people in the group, including myself. I was greatly touched by Evi kneeling before me and thanking me for leaving my own country and family to serve God in her nation. The prophecies were so encouraging that, by the time I left, I felt quite rejuvenated. Years of weariness had just washed away and hope had sprung up afresh as we basked in the presence of the Holy Spirit. This was to be far from the last time I would join together with George and Evi. Yet there was to be another, different link, which would also provide some new direction.

It was the summer prior to setting up the prayer chain, that I was given a book that would become very special to me in God's leading. It was called *The Grace Outpouring* by Roy Godwin and was given to me by a couple we knew on Paros. They had a house out in the countryside and, like many Greek houses, the local cat population had homed in on them as a good source of food. Surrounded by open fields and with several chicken coops supplying a steady flow of grain, there were mice and rats around in plenty. A cat – or several cats – was essential to keep the mice population under control. Peter had kindly offered to feed the cats during the winter, so we had become friends, sharing dinners together from time to time. On one such occasion, Mary handed me the book, which was about a place in the Welsh National Park called Ffald-Y-Brenin, meaning "The Sheepfold of the King".

Many outstanding miracles had occurred there, due to the presence of God in response to the daily worship and prayer going on. People would start praying a simple grace prayer over their food and suddenly hours would have passed, they'd missed their planned walk and it was midnight. Although I read many books about such outpourings of the Holy Spirit around the world and heard about many others on the Christian TV Channels, I rarely felt led to actually go and visit the places. This particular book had so touched me that, in 2013, I had taught in our Sunday group on the things happening there. The very next Sunday, having travelled to my sister's church in England, I was surprised to find Ffald-Y-Brenin suddenly being mentioned by Rob, the pastor of her church. He hadn't preached that Sunday but, at the end of the service, he felt he had to share the story of Roy Godwin's dramatic, miraculous healing of his leg. I had never heard the story as it wasn't recorded in the book I had read. Roy Godwin had been in a car accident with his family and he had severely broken his leg. The bones were shattered into so many pieces that the doctors said they couldn't possibly set the leg and they would have to amputate it. Roy Godwin asked for time to pray about it, and the Lord told him not to allow the amputation because He was going to heal him. Roy refused the amputation and, during his two months in hospital, the Lord completely healed the leg. I was astonished that Pastor Rob should choose to share this story the Sunday after I had taught on Ffald-Y-Brenin, and again it seemed like a confirmation that God was leading me to go to the place.

I was completely taken aback to learn that Hal and Mary, who had given me the book, also had a holiday home in Wales only a few miles from Ffald-Y-Brenin! "We rent it out all around the year, but if you go out of season, you can stay there free". It seemed March was a quiet time for them and I could stay then. What a generous offer.

So this was how it came about that I was browsing the Internet to see what the March temperatures were like in Wales. I struggle with the cold in Greece when the temperature falls below 15C, after the summer 28–35C, so I knew I couldn't handle 5C too well. Ffald-Y-Brenin was an old stone built farm that had been converted into a residential prayer retreat and I couldn't count on there being much heating. Half the point of going was to be able to enjoy the presence of God in the Welsh outdoors, as many people had had profound meetings with God, just sitting at the foot of the large wooden cross overlooking the valley. I wanted to go at a time of year when I could do that without shivering to my bones. With the temperatures in March ranging from 2–10 C, I knew there was absolutely no chance of me going then; I'd freeze in that. May was the earliest possibility, 5–16C, or preferably June at 9–19C; that I could cope with. I'd just have to forgo the offer of free accommodation in Newport and see what I could find locally. The accommodation at Ffald-Y-Brenin was fully booked for the whole year, a good indication of the popularity of the place. In the end, I tried the list of Bed and Breakfast farmhouses supplied by Ffald-Y-Brenin and landed on a real little gem. Lilwen McAllister had won the AA Bed and Breakfast of the year award and, after I had reserved a room for the week, I realised she was mentioned in the book *The Grace Outpouring*. The theme at Ffald-Y-Brenin is to pray blessings over people, including those from the local area school, farms and businesses. As a result of her marvellous guest house, wonderful breakfasts, plus the blessings prayers, she had been awarded five stars and the landlady of the year award. I would find out when I got there exactly why she had won it. I booked it for six nights as I wanted to have plenty of time to soak in the presence of God. I planned to travel there on Sunday, 1 June, to be ready for five days of heaven from Monday to Friday. Then, I would tear myself away to go back to the real world and visit my sister and niece before returning to Greece.

Sitting on the train, before I even got to Ffald-Y-Brenin, I heard God speak to me so clearly:

"I am taking you to this place Ffald-Y-Brenin to prepare you, to build you up for what is to come, to make you a part of a team of warriors".

I arrived at Erw Lon Farmhouse, Lilwen's place, at around three in the afternoon. She very kindly picked me up from the station, so I hadn't had to search for a taxi. My room was a sheer delight, with embroidered pillowcases and duvet cover, matching curtains and wallpaper, masses of wardrobe space in lovely, white, fitted units and most important of all, central heating and a kettle to make hot drinks.

I had planned to spend the rest of the day relaxing, but God had another plan. After a lovely sandwich, cake and coffee in the lounge, Lilwen insisted on driving me up to Ffald-Y-Brenin, "since that's what you came for", as she put it. I was delighted to accept her offer and off we went through the glorious, country lanes in her sleek, black BMW, along a narrow one-track road. As she dropped me off, she kindly asked what time I would like her to pick me up.

The place was beautiful, with old stone buildings, perfectly maintained gardens and lawns, and it was so homely. I made my way to the little, round, stone chapel: this was where many people had had remarkable encounters with God. I arrived to find a group of Americans in there. It was in between the regular times of prayer and this group were spontaneously worshipping and ministering to each other. Then the eldest lady, who was

German but lived in America, started to prophesy to different members of the group. I just sat quietly, basking in the presence of God, taking in all that was going on around me. She then came over to me and began to prophesy over me. Now, please remember, this lady had never set eyes on me before this moment.

"That I have promised will come about. God will take you to other places and you will merely WALK, PRAY AND ANOINT WITH OIL. You have been faithful. There are people God will show you, who you will claim for the kingdom of God. Don't underestimate what is inside of you".

Now what this lady didn't know was that, about two months earlier, on one of my normal daily one hour walks through the village and across the fields, I had felt God say to me that I was to walk around the village and to pray for the people. At the time I wasn't sure that it was God speaking, perhaps it was just me thinking to do it. So I had asked God if it was Him speaking to me to do this, He would confirm it somehow. Well, if this wasn't a confirmation, I don't know what else would be! How amazing! Thinking about the logistics of what had just happened: God had flown me in from Greece; told me the week to come; organised getting me there one day earlier than I had planned, and brought this woman from California at precisely the same moment. As the group left the chapel later in the afternoon, I understood that they were only there for this one day, so if I had waited until the Monday, I would have missed her and God's answer to my request. Interestingly, as well as the prophecy, her husband came to sit with me. He took my hand, which I thought was rather sweet of him. Amongst the things he told me was that his wife, Marlis, had been part of the team that had gone to Mount Everest, as related in the very book by Peter Wagner which I had read earlier. I was astonished! What an amazing lady God had sent to prophesy over me. I was deeply touched. Now I knew at least a part of why God had led me to this place at this time. There was more to come later in the week.

The reason I had chosen to come during the first week of the month was that, on the first Tuesday of each month, Ffald-Y-Brenin have a monthly prayer day which includes worship, teaching, prayer, ministry and good fellowship. The meeting is held in a large church hall in the valley, amongst lush green fields where cows graze peacefully at the side of a slowly meandering river. I had refused Lilwen's offer of a lift as it was a lovely walk down from the farm. I had no idea what Roy Godwin looked like and was quite surprised to discover that he was the rather unassuming gentleman at the front playing the piano for worship. He invited all the people who were there from countries outside the UK to stand and introduce themselves. There were some from Singapore, Mozambique and other really far away places, as well as me from Greece. When I introduced myself as coming from Greece, Roy immediately said, "Oh, you need to meet that couple over there; they are going to Greece". Then he added, "Well, why don't the three of you come to the front and we'll pray for you."

So there it was; God wanted a roomful of maybe two hundred people to pray for the three of us and Greece. It seemed I had got God's timing right, even if He had to make me feel March was way too cold for a visit. The couple were due to leave for Greece the following Saturday. They were going to seek God's leading as to where He wanted to start a TransMed House of Prayer. TransMed was a vision to plant Missional Houses of Prayer around the Mediterranean. They only had one contact on Crete and, six months earlier, I had only the name of one contact there, but no phone number. Now, because one of the ladies in our church group had left to work in Crete for the summer, I had several names and phone numbers of churches there to share with them. I felt like a messenger sent by God to help establish a House of Prayer on that island. If I had indeed heard God correctly on the journey down to Wales, and if I was to be part of a "Team of warriors", He certainly was giving me the contacts and strategy.

The rest of the day passed happily with excellent teaching by different guest speakers. A Welsh lady, Dr. Rhiannon Lloyd gave a very moving teaching on "Healing, Forgiveness and Reconciliation" based on her work in Liberia, Rwanda, Congo and Kenya. Repeatedly, when God instructed her to go to strife-torn places, she would ask Him what one woman alone could do in such places. On one such occasion God replied, "I can use you, just one woman, because you go in as a child."

God was looking for someone naïve enough to do what others knew couldn't be done. Her humility was touching. God had used her to bring reconciliation in seemingly hopeless situations. The ability of God to use just one woman was a great source of encouragement to me. The whole teaching was freely available on the Internet on *lerucher.org*, so that evening, on returning to my room, I was able to settle down and read more of her amazing work on my mini-laptop. I sat with my feet on the radiator, snuggled up warmly, delighting in the freedom from the everyday things of life that jostle for one's time in a normal day at home.

In my week at Ffald-Y-Brenin I spent hours in the chapel, resting in the presence of God. They have a daily rhythm of prayer there with four sessions starting at 9:30, 12:45, 17:00 and 22:00. Lilwen ran me up in the car each day to be in time for the 9:30 morning prayer. I had decided against fasting, since her breakfasts were much of the reason she had won her AA five stars. Every morning, she presented me with a beautiful, extremely large, bowl of fresh fruit salad with more than ten varieties of fruit: strawberries, raspberries, grapes and plums, amongst others. There was enough for two people, but I gladly ate most of it. There were cereals as well, and all before the traditional English breakfast of bacon and eggs, sausage, mushrooms and tomatoes. On alternate days, I opted for smoked haddock – something you can't find at all on a Greek island – which had always been a favourite of mine. Both options were served with a pot of piping hot coffee, toast and jam, and fresh cream. It was like paradise. It was just as well I didn't eat much the rest of the day, or I would have put on even more weight than I did.

Arriving at the chapel each morning, we were usually a group of ten to twenty-five people. We worshipped, read standard readings from the Bible, and prayed together. Sometimes the prayers were for individuals, other times for nations and, of course, for Wales. Just by listening, I learnt how to pray blessings over individuals, people groups, governments and nations.

I would then spend the mornings in the chapel, in silence, mostly alone with God, although occasional visitors were shown around by the Ffald-Y-Brenin staff. After the shorter midday prayer at 12:45, I would go to the coffee lounge from where there were magnificent views down the valley and to the wooden cross. I met such a variety of people from different nations and began to understand that many people or couples had started the daily rhythm of prayer with just two or three people. There was no prerequisite to have a large group. One couple I met told me how they do the morning prayer in bed with their cup of tea before they even get up, and then the night prayer in bed with their cup of cocoa. A lady who lived alone followed the prayer rhythm daily, so we prayed together that God would send her someone to pray with her. It showed that God could use someone in this way even if they were alone.

In the afternoon when it wasn't raining, I walked down to the cross to sit and enjoy the open countryside, but people sometimes commented on how I was always dressed in a big jacket, jumper and my black beret, as they skipped around in their much lighter clothing. What they didn't know was that I also had on my thermal underwear! It had been 28C when I had left Greece and it was only 16C there – distinctly chilly to me!

Each day, I was able to join the afternoon prayer at 17:00, before Lilwen or her husband picked me up and took me back to the farm for the evening. The six days were simply glorious. Even though I had been unable to have accommodation at Ffald-Y-Brenin, thus missing the fellowship of the meals together with the other residents, I probably was able to spend more time alone with God by staying at the farm. I was more than happy.

As a result of making the contact with the couple going to Crete, I was then led to another Ffald-Y-Brenin couple that they were meeting up with when they got there. Simon and Katie had a yacht and were sailing around the Greek islands simply praying blessings over the people and the islands. We made contact by email, and I said that they would be very welcome to come down to Paros for a visit. They replied that they didn't think they could make it in 2014, but maybe the next year. We left it at that.

In the meantime, I set up a Ffald-Y-Brenin style prayer room in the West Wing next to the olive grove. Peter made a large wooden cross for it; there were chairs and cushions on boxes to sit on, squashed between the 300 Christian books, videos and DVDs. All we needed now was some people who would be willing to pray regularly.

It came as quite a surprise when, around September, I suddenly received an email from Simon and Katie saying they were coming after all. I had given them directions to our local harbour of Piso Livadi, so was quite surprised when I received a phone call on a Monday to say that they were in Naoussa, on the far side of the island. The wind had been so strong that they had failed to find Piso Livadi, so had settled on Naoussa, which they knew from a previous visit.

We made our first contact at Monastiri beach, where they had moored close to the shore so their dog could walk on dry land twice a day, as dogs need to do. Katie and I spent two hours sharing some of what God had done in our lives, while Simon stayed on board to ensure the anchor held and the yacht was safe in the raging storm. As we talked, the wind was so strong that the paper cover on my iced coffee cup blew away, but we talked on; there was so much to discover.

Since even stronger force seven winds were forecast and their first mooring was quite exposed, they decided to come over to Piso Livadi on the Thursday, before the bad weather set in. This was much more practical as it was so close to us. Then, they could join us on the Sunday and meet the people in our group. Another bonus was discovering that mooring was free of charge since the extended harbour had been built with an EU grant to promote tourism. For just five euros they were able to hook up to water and electricity. By the Saturday, it was lashing with rain and the shelter of the harbour was most welcome. Even so, it was still wild and as I lay in my bed on dry land, I wondered how anyone could possibly sleep on a yacht in a storm like that.

On the Sunday when we met together, I was able to give a teaching on the concept of praying blessings over people and areas, and then Katie and Simon talked about how they put this into practice. What a great way to live.

The weather continued to be awful from a sailor's point of view. Yes, it was clear blue sky and sunshine, but the wind was much too strong to risk trying to return to Poros, their base island. I was going to have to leave them on Paros for two days while I flew to Athens for my six monthly check-up with the oncologist. The bad weather ensured that they would still be in the harbour on my return.

Just prior to Simon and Katie's visit to Paros, we had also arranged for George and Evi Markakis from the Athens Shalom Prayer Centre to come down to us for a few days. The purpose of the visit was to join us in prayer, then to give us advice on how we might be able to make our prayer more effective and to give us further teaching as required. I also wanted them to use their gifts of spiritual discernment to evaluate the spiritual atmosphere over the island. They arrived on a Wednesday at the end of August. Much to my surprise, in spite of a very heavily booked European schedule, they were able to stay with us for five days through to the Monday evening ferry. This meant that not only could they observe and advise at our Thursday weekly prayer meeting, but George could also teach at our Sunday meeting and meet the entire group. He would even still have time to give me some additional teaching and ministry advice. It was a wonderful time of refreshment for me.

At the Thursday meeting, George and Evi observed as they joined us in worship and prayer, and then gave us the feedback we had requested. George explained that the reason we have been so exhausted by prayer and feeling weighed down was because all our prayer meetings had been intercessory prayer meetings. He explained that we also needed to have times where we met to worship and to be refreshed in the presence of God. We could also seek the Holy Spirit to prophesy over each other for our strengthening, encouragement and comfort. (1 Corinthians 14:3). Our worship and intercession is all well and good and it is wonderful to have had such a thing going on every week for years, but to be able to keep going we also need the times of refreshment.

The next day, we were able to have a second prayer meeting led by George, in order for us to observe and learn. Sensitive to the leading of the Holy Spirit, he felt that first we needed to offer each other forgiveness – a very bold thing to tell us – which we then did, each confessing the problems we had with one another. The need for this and confession to each other of our sins was something God had been showing me through the book *High Level Warfare Safe from Counter-attacks* by Ana Mendez

Ferrell. This then removes the enemy's authority to attack us. He taught how the atmosphere of the island affects us, and how we need to identify with it and say Lord forgive us on Paros, not Lord forgive them. We also needed to learn that if we are unclean, we are not allowed into the camp of God, so then we drift away from His refreshing and we are consequently in the desert.

As we left the meeting to return to Logaras, George spotted a sign to a sanctuary of Apollo, quite close to Annamarie's house. Paros has a wealth of such ancient, archaeological sites. These sites, which were previously places of worship to pagan Greek gods, such as Apollo, Athena and Asclepios, are used as gates to the enemy until they are dealt with spiritually. We climbed up the narrow path flanked by dry stone walls and, on arrival at the top, we worshipped our Lord God and prayed in tongues. We did not bind or loose in Jesus' name (that is: to forbid or to permit something to happen); we simply worshipped the Lord.

On Saturday, George felt that he had to go to a particular Greek church in the capital town of the island (but not the main church) to continue the process. It is close to another ancient sanctuary of Apollo Pythios and Asclepios. There were a profusion of dragons in the décor, even on the door handles. In the book of Revelation in the Bible, a dragon is a symbol of Satan, as is a snake. (This is why I won't have anything in our house with pictures of dragons or snakes on it, not even Chinese noodles packets, or bags from the chemist with a symbol of Asclepios.)

While George was doing the spiritual work, I hit the kitchen to prepare food for about ten people who we expected at our Sunday Worship meeting. Then we needed to go into the main town ourselves to pick up my niece arriving on the *High Speed* ferry from Mykonos for her annual holiday.

It was a wonderful crowd that gathered that Sunday morning. We had visitors from Hellenic Ministries,

German Karen, and Australian Martha, who had last visited us in 2004 for the Hellenic Ministries Bible distribution, prayer and evangelism during the Olympic Games. George led and taught on: "Taste and see that the Lord is good" Psalm 34:8. We each responded by sharing one good thing that God had done for us. That then gave us an illustration of how we can have faith for God to do something good today. Everyone stayed for lunch, which was a joyful occasion. We all sat at a long table on the terrace outdoors, enjoying the fabulous August weather.

By the time evening came, it was tempting to rest, but I still had a long list of questions and was eager to make the most of George's visit. Who knew how long it would be before I would have the opportunity again? I left Peter watching the Belgian weekly sports program and crossed the road to the rooms where George and Evi were staying. Their room had a larger than average balcony and a lovely view across the olive grove to the sea and to Naxos. We talked of the role of priests and warriors in the church as an army keeping rank, enquiring of the Lord, warfare and waiting, amongst other things. Interestingly, in recent weeks and for the first time ever, I had been looking at Ley lines on Google. George also brought up the subject and defined Ley lines as "Geo-spiritual routes/structures of transference of spiritual power and influence". Over Paros, there are Ley lines in a triangle from the Peloponnese to Tinos and down to Knossos in Crete. Fascinatingly, many of the places Simon and Katie have been led to visit to pray are within this triangle. I wondered if this could be God's strategy. Other information we discussed was that the goddess Athena was the protector of Paros and that, in ancient times, there was a large temple to her in the main town. The Cretan Bull of Knossos was worship to Zeus.

There can be no doubt that since George and Evi prayed and visited some of these ancient places of worship there has been a distinct lightening of the spiritual atmosphere, which upon arrival they had discerned to be "as heavy as glue"! Prayer is not such hard work; worship seems more intimate with the presence and peace of God coming as we speak and share with unsaved.

It wasn't to be that long before I would visit them again at their home outside Athens as I needed to make my next six-monthly hospital check-up. Something very special would happen on that visit as we worshipped together. I travelled up to Athens a month later, having done the battery of tests and checks on Paros, the results of which I needed to take with me for the oncologist. It was a younger doctor again, the senior specialist had long moved on to greater things than check-ups. After carefully checking the results of my blood tests, an ultrasound on my abdomen and two chest X-rays, he proceeded with the normal physical examination of my breasts; well, my one remaining breast, my armpits and neck. I decided to ask him the million dollar question.

"Well, doctor, after me first having breast cancer twenty years ago, with surgery but no chemotherapy, radiotherapy, or medication at that time, then breast cancer again in 2010, followed by chemotherapy, radiotherapy and Tamoxifen, would you say that I am a walking miracle?"

He looked thoughtful and replied, "Yes, you could say that. You are certainly very lucky to be alive".

"Well doctor, I don't think it's anything to do with luck rather that I'm very blessed to have been given the gift of faith in the healing power of Jesus Christ, who forgives all my sins and heals all my diseases". Understandably, he looked a bit taken aback, but if I have had to suffer all this, the least I can do is to use my suffering as a vehicle to preach the gospel. Even the apostle Paul said, "It was because of an illness that I first preached the gospel to you."

So, with the doctor agreeing, as closely as it is possible to get a doctor to agree that I am a walking miracle, I skipped along to George and Evi's home feeling very peaceful. We enjoyed a lovely lunch, and then George spent the afternoon teaching me little gems from his vast knowledge on subjects I had barely touched on in my thirty years as a Christian. I asked George if he regularly went to the sanctuaries of ancient Greek gods and goddesses to pray and lift up the name of Jesus, as he had done on Paros. "I mean the Acropolis in Athens and such-like?" He just smiled and replied that he had done this hundreds of times.

The evening was to be different to the last time I visited. Another couple, Nikos and Kalia had come to join us at the house rather than driving down to the Shalom centre. We would worship together at the house and see where the Holy Spirit would lead us. Nikos played guitar and we worshipped, sometimes in English and sometimes in Greek. After more than an hour, George asked if anyone had received anything from God. Evi and George shared some things and then he asked me had I received anything.

"Well, yes I did, I had a vision, which is pretty unusual for me. In the vision, I was driving along a straight tarmac road in the countryside. Then, suddenly, there was a small slip-road off to the left which sloped down into a beautiful green field. The car continued to drive across the grass, not slowing down at all. The field was full of pink flowers and, as the car went along, the pink flowers were cascading all over the car and the windscreen. I don't know what it means or who it is for, but I understand that cars in dreams and visions denote ministries and buses symbolize churches."

George explained that the vision was definitely for me and that the green fields indicated prosperity, something fresh and joyful. Evi felt that the pink flowers indicated something very feminine. The fact that the car went off the track, indicated that the ministry would be something unusual. I had a really happy, expectant feeling about the whole thing. It was way past midnight when I finally went to bed.

The next morning, I remembered a dream I had had years ago, also about a car. It must have been around 2009, before I discovered I had cancer in my second breast and before the chemotherapy. I was in a car driving up the hill from Piso Livadi harbour to Logaras beach. In front of me was a bus and all the people from the church were in the bus. I couldn't understand why I was in the car alone and not in the bus with the others. Then, suddenly, the bus began to roll down the hill towards me, completely out of control. I had to rapidly reverse my car down the hill and I finally came to a stop in the car park at the bottom. The car park, which in reality is black tarmac, in the dream was dry, cracked mud like you would see in a desert drought. On telling George about the earlier dream, he said that now the latest vision made more sense. The first dream was foretelling of a great time of difficulty and dryness in the ministry on Paros. This was in fact the case in 2010, as I went through months of treatment and chemotherapy. Now, the vision of the green field, in contrast, was telling of a time of great blessing and prosperity.

In the weeks that followed, I couldn't help thinking about the pink flowers. I kept thinking of the pink bow which is the symbol of safety in breast cancer advertising. There certainly wasn't anything much more feminine than a woman's breast. I was inclined to think that this was a foretelling of my long awaited restoration. Interestingly, George and Evi had planned a three-day conference in December. The theme was "Kingdom, Power and Healing". Would God choose this event to fulfil His promise of restoration to me? December 2014 would be exactly twenty years since the removal of my left breast.

Another interesting thing was that a lady who had visited me in the hospital twenty years ago had just found me again and contacted me for prayer. I had not seen or heard from her in all that time, yet here she was and thinking of coming to the meetings for healing from pancreatitis. Could God have called her onto the scene as she had been a witness to the removal of my breast, as well as to completely heal her and remove the gallbladder stones? After all, it was to be a conference on healing. I pondered all these things in my heart and decided I would share them with the people on the prayer chain.

At the December conference, there were people there from many nations: Italy, Romania, Bulgaria, England, Austria, as well as Greece. Several of us, as pastors, had been asked to share what God was doing in our cities and churches. I was also invited to serve Communion on Sunday with an Italian man, a clear message of affirmation that this group of Christians recognised the ministry of women in the church. We worshipped in English, Greek, Bulgarian and German. It was a glorious experience, the room filled with either the rich sound of the keyboards, or the gentle ripple of guitar, windpipes and mandolin. Our voices soared in joy or were hushed to a whisper as the Holy Spirit fell and drew us into the presence of the King. What a feast compared to our simple worship on Paros. I know that God is pleased with it all, but it seemed like the difference between the simple chorus of a child and the chorus of angels in heaven around the throne. People were then invited to share what they had seen or heard in the spirit as they had worshipped. It was like a rainbow of visions had been showered amongst those present.

George explained that Shalom Centre saw its ministry as helping others to meet with the Lord. Some of us had been asked to share what God was doing in our lives and identify any special areas for prayer. I related what God had done on Paros; how it was all supernatural, from his original call to bring me there to bringing us a steady stream of people from all nations. I shared my surprise that, though I had expected to reach Greek people for Him, in reality they had been in the minority until now.

I also felt I had to tell of the opposition we had experienced from other churches and how the forces of darkness had tried to take me out with cancer of the left breast in 1994 and again in the right breast in 2010. Glory to God, I was alive and well, healed in Jesus' name. It seemed right to even share that I continued to believe the promise of the restoration of my breast, and that since it was exactly twenty years to the month maybe this could be God's time. I knew that I was surrounded by family, people of the same spirit who would believe with me and no doubt pray for me, as I would for them.

As I listened to others speak, I became aware that many of these people were only small groups. In Rome they had started with nine, in Luton they were a watchman outpost of just three, in New York four, yet God was using each group to fulfil His divine purpose, creating an army of prayer warriors around the world.

In the afternoon, there was a time of ordaining ministers, two in a group in Halkidiki, Robert from the Luton group and Nikos, there at Shalom in Athens. Nikos had taken the bold step of faith to leave Germany, where he had a secure job with an income, to come to Athens to serve the Lord. It was a time to affirm and recognise what God was doing through them. As George, Evi and the ministers of Shalom laid hands on them, I knew in my heart that this was where we belonged. Those in our group on Paros had recently agreed that I should assume the title of pastor and I had accepted. I knew there was a need to complete the process by the laying on of hands to ordain me, but I kept it to myself. We had studied the Word extensively regarding the role of women in the church and it was very evident from the original Greek, that Chloe and Phoebe were the leaders of the early churches that met in their homes. Even the Modern Greek had been altered to hide this fact to protect the male domination of the church.

Late in the evening, after we all had dinner together, George confirmed this inner witness of the Spirit by calling me to one side and asking me if I felt ready to be ordained by them. I knew the answer was yes, but asked for time to pray about it overnight. It was with this background to events that, on the Sunday afternoon, George, Evi and the other ministers in the church affirmed me as the pastor of the Paros church group and laid hands on me in the same way that Barnabas and Saul were commissioned in Acts 13 for the work to which the Lord had called them. At last, we were a part of a bigger family, no longer isolated and separated from the main body of Christ in Greece.

The teaching on Sunday was on healing, the final part of our conference theme of "Kingdom, Power, Healing". Angeliki, the pastor of Shalom, had written seven scriptures on the flip chart but, due to shortness of time, had not taught on them, as she had originally intended. She graciously stepped down to allow the next speaker from Romania more time. Imagine Marian Zamfir's surprise when he saw on the flip chart the very seven scriptures he had been led to teach on.

"It's a miracle," he declared, and we all laughed at the provision and encouragement of God to help him teach in English, not his native tongue. He taught on seven things that can block healing that we need to deal with before actually praying for a person's healing: ignorance of healing, unbelief, unconfessed sin, unforgiveness, occult involvement, wrong covenants such as Freemasonry and, finally, demons. We were truly blessed by his teaching and the stories of those healed. His challenge to us was to always ask others in need, "Did you pray? No? Then can I pray for you?"

It was not that I had not heard such a seven point teaching before as I had often ministered to people in this way, but God wanted it all fresh in my mind because, when the conference ended that evening, he had a job for me to do. Marian called those who wanted prayer for healing forward. I gladly took the opportunity in view of my expectancy of the final restoration of my breast, but it was not to be at that time. I thought that I would return to my hotel room and bask in the presence of God for hours before sleeping. Who knows? It could easily manifest in the stillness alone with my Jesus.

I returned to my hotel room to find a message at reception. Libby, the lady I had not seen for twenty years, had telephoned to arrange to meet. I called her and she said that she would arrive in half an hour. I just had time to change out of the formal, blue business skirt and jacket I was wearing and slip into some more comfortable shoes and trousers.

On her arrival, we chose to remain in my room and I made coffee. I listened to her recount various things that had happened over the last twenty years. It was clear that she required ministry for some emotional hurts, and I needed to lead her in prayer to be sure that she had no unforgiveness in her heart as a result of these. It seemed best to lead Libby in a prayer of repentance to receive Christ as her Lord and Saviour. I then was able to lay hands on her in Jesus' name for healing from pancreatitis, a gallbladder full of stones, fibromyalgia and osteoarthritis. Prior to the prayer, she had been having a great deal of difficulty eating and had lost a lot of weight, but in the weeks that followed she was able to eat and had gained a few kilos. At a party she even decided to try pizza and black forest gateau and was able to enjoy it, glory to God.

It was a happy Barbara that returned to Paros the next day; I may not have received my restoration, but, for sure, Libby got a significant part of hers! She immediately started reading her Bible for the first time in many years and became very excited about what it said, even the book of Job! It was a great pleasure to me to hear what she was reading and how it was helping her.

It therefore came as quite a surprise, when I visited her at the end of March, to discover that she was again suffering pain and burning every time she ate something, even just dry toast and tea. It was time to dig down to the root of the problem. As we talked and looked at her old photograph album, it transpired that her Father had been a Freemason. Although the Freemasons do many charitable deeds and are thought to be an honourable institution, what is unknown to many people is that Freemasonry has its roots in the worship of god called Jahbulon. Jahbulon is mostly referred to as "the Great Architect of the Universe", and this is where the deception comes in. Jahbulon is a composite name from Jaweh, the God of the Hebrews, (which is good), but also Bul from Baal, the ancient Canaanite fertility god, and On from Osiris, the ancient Egyptian god of the underworld. In view of God's command: "You shall have no other gods before me", this worship of Canaanite and Egyptian gods was forbidden. It was because my father had been a Freemason that I was only too aware of the problems that this could bring to a whole family.

Her mother had worked in an old people's home and had joined in séances in the evenings with the other staff. The Bible expressly forbids the use of mediums to contact the dead, as King Saul found out to his cost when he contacted the prophet, Samuel.

While we were talking, I also noticed a collection of Greek icons on a table in the corner of the room. Idolatry is expressly forbidden in the Bible.

So there we had at least three areas to start with that would have brought a curse on the family line. Again it was necessary to lead someone in Jesus' name through the seven steps to release from curses. These would be responsible not just for her ill-health, but also for her difficult financial situation and various other negative things happening in her life. Libby understood immediately and determined to get rid of the icons, which she did the same day. I then prayed for her healing and that she would be able to sleep. She had been unable to sleep for weeks because of the pain and would rarely sleep more than a few hours, usually in the early hours of the morning after a tortuous night.

The next morning, she awoke after ten hours undisturbed sleep and the pain had subsided. Unfortunately, the pain returned when she ate that day so, later in the week, in desperation, she went to the hospital. The doors which had previously been firmly shut were opened and surgery was scheduled for the end of the month. Healing through doctors is just as much a healing as an instant miracle, even though we would all prefer the painless miracle.

It seemed good to notify the whole prayer chain of the problems she was having. After doing this, it became evident that, within one hour of the email winging its way on the internet, she was already feeling better and, two days later there was a significant improvement.

Such is often the case, releasing people from curses. It is sometimes a one-off prayer of release and the problem is solved, as it was with Amy in Colorado. For others, it is rather like an octopus sitting on their back and we need to pry off the legs one at a time. I felt sure that Libby would eventually be set free and blossom like a rose. Since curses can be self-imposed, it is of paramount importance that she learns not to speak negative words over herself.

As 2014 ended, I felt that we had made important links with others in the body of Christ. In just one year God had led us to make contact with The Shalom Prayer Centre in Athens, the Athens Passage to Life group for drug and alcohol related problems, and Simon and Katie with their yacht, who are linked to Ffald-Y-Brenin in Wales. We had also set up our prayer chain, which included people in the USA, Canada, Australia, England, Germany, Norway and Greece. Finally, after twenty-five years, we were being built into an army of people that could serve God and help many others. We would, no doubt, find out what God had planned in all of this.

A lot had changed since those early days alone when I had first arrived in the Land Rover. God had indeed fulfilled His promise to send me *to Greece and the distant islands* to proclaim His glory, as I relate in my first book of that name. The miracle of the five-drachma coin had provided money to complete the purchase of the land for a home on Paros. God's promise had included not just a home but a husband. Yes, there had been many opportunities to proclaim His glory; for sure there would be many more.

17 THE GREEK CRISIS

My trips to Athens were profoundly disturbing. While walking around the back streets near Omonia Square, it was all too common to find people of all ages lying on cardboard cartons, the lucky ones under blankets. Some were there because they had addictions to drugs or alcohol: the silent thief stealing from them every few euros they could scrape together. Others were there because they had lost their jobs and couldn't pay their rent; they had simply been put on the streets. Exasperated landlords struggling themselves to pay the barrage of new property taxes were in danger of having their property confiscated if they didn't cough up the new *Enfia* property tax. Tenants who paid their rent had to be given priority over those who couldn't.

For the Passage to Life Group, this was their backyard and their opportunity to minister to the lost and the needy. All year round at night they were out on the streets in teams serving hot tea and croissants to those desperate souls; in winter, distributing blankets, hats and gloves. Other nights they were in a central park, *Pedion tou Areos*, where many homeless people and drug addicts slept on benches or huddled together in corners. Not only did they offer them temporary relief on the street, but they also offered a rescue program to drug addicts who wanted to be set free. They had a central building with accommodation and cooking facilities for addicts who were prepared to leave the questionable freedom of the park and to join the group on a residential basis. Throughout the week, those on the program would be led to understand that only with the help of God Himself could they be truly set free. Prayer and Bible reading became a central part of their life and, as they progressed, they would join the teams going out nightly to help others.

Most of the Greeks in Athens and the islands are home owners so, at least when times became hard for them, they have a roof over their heads. Traditionally, property has always been passed down the family line and, in the past, was rarely sold. For those without inherited homes from grandma, it was a different story. More and more people were losing their jobs – some 30,000 in January alone – and those who had taken mortgages were having their homes repossessed by the banks. Greek people were regularly to be seen searching through the dumper rubbish bins in search of discarded pizza or items past their sell-by date.

The cuts to the pensions at the lower end of the scale were truly tragic. It had become common for pensioners to suffer the loss of hundreds of euros a month and if someone only had six hundred euros a month to live on, cutting it to less that five hundred was a disaster. We knew of whole families where three generations were trying to eke out a living on granddad's pension: the sons and daughters had lost their jobs or were never able to get one in the first place. In the 18–30 age groups, unemployment is currently running at fifty percent.

Friends and visiting tourists would regularly ask us what the situation on the islands was like. Was it really as bad as they had seen on European news channels? To understand the island situation, one really has to have lived on one to fully understand the family background. On Paros, the average Greek family owns two or three homes, inherited from grandma, mum and dad or Aunty Maria. One of these is often an apartment in Athens. The retention of this is considered essential for the grown up children to attend university or the occasional family visits to Athens or hospitals, and as the winter residence to escape from the seventy to eighty percent humidity. Beach side property locations provide the base for the tourist related business of rooms or restaurants, while the central village house provides neighbours and much needed company during the winter months, when not in Athens.

Many of the local people have their own olive grove and *perivoli*, the Greek vegetable garden. Chicken runs are common and some even extend their farmer status to include turkey, geese and ducks. Our neighbours also have their own sheep and goats. If people don't have their own, then someone in the family probably will, even a remote second cousin. In this environment, when faced with a pension cut or the loss of a job, if you have olive oil, eggs, and a wonderful supply of onions, garlic, tomatoes, peppers, courgettes, aubergines, plus trees full of lemons, mandarins and oranges, life is still quite manageable. For those with the sheep and goats, there is continual fresh milk and cheese, and lamb and goat in plenty, especially for the Easter feast; add to this their own vineyards for wine and life can even be cheerful.

Many of these same people have their own rooms, often between ten and twenty in number. Even with a reduction in tourism over the last years, the income at 30–50 euros a room for the months of July and August alone will supplement the local food supply nicely. It is true that the taxes that owners now have to pay have significantly increased, which all adds to the pervading atmosphere of gloom. The concept of paying thirty percent taxes on one's earnings, as we did for years in England and Belgium, is shocking to the Greek mind after years of paying almost no taxes at all. Of course, you will always be told that they still have three empty rooms in August when, in the old days, they would have been full, but that is just an interestingly Greek attribute. A Greek will rarely admit how well they are doing; after all, one doesn't want to encourage jealously and attract the evil eye!

So is anyone suffering on the Greek Islands? Yes, indeed they are, but it is mostly the foreigners who came from Albania, Bulgaria and Poland, along with the English and Germans. These people are in the trap of needing to pay rent. Many have been forced to work in the black market, where IKA national insurance is not paid. Alternatively, they have to pay it themselves out of an already low wage. People are working full time cleaning rooms, on building sites and even in national supermarkets for only 500 euros a month or less. When the work dries up, or their employers tell them they have no money to pay them so they will have to wait, a return to their homeland has become an increasingly common necessity. We live in a nation where fifty percent of the youth are unemployed, but almost all the cleaning of hotels and rooms is done by non-nationals!

Swedish Sven was a foreign hopeful who had come to Greece to start a new life. His situation when he finally lost his job, couldn't pay his rent and had no family support is a stark contrast to the Greek family support system. The depression and all too common escape route of drinking *suma* to drown his sorrows had taken its grip. We had sponsored him to join the Athens Passage to Life program to break his addictions. After eighteen months on the program and without a drink, the question was where and what could he do to go back into the world and be self sufficient. Workwise in Athens, it was dire. On Paros, the supply of appropriate work for him had more or less dried up, and the temptation to return to his old watering holes could prove too much of a temptation. I was reluctant to help him return to Paros in view of the potential danger. So it was with great joy that God opened a door for him to join a ministry in Ireland. Drop In Ministries have around thirty second hand shops in Ireland. The clothes and furniture sold provides money to support people in need around the world. Sven was invited to join them and live in Ballyards castle, a residential centre used for Christian Conferences. Sven spends his time maintaining the premises and making himself useful with the catering for the weekend conferences. He recently attended a discipleship training course, which will equip him to further serve the ministry. Local Parians who knew Sven are astonished at the change in his situation; a wonderful illustration of how much God can change a life and a person's circumstances if they will just open the door and let Him come in.

Drop In Ministries have recently announced that they will have a full time presence in Athens to help the refugees, which is a crisis of epic proportions. Those previously trapped in their own war torn countries have been brought to the very doorstep of Greece. Many who were never free to hear the gospel of Jesus Christ are now free to listen and choose. It is an enormous opportunity for this Christian nation, the European birth place of Christianity.

Here on Paros, we have long had our links with another organisation in Greece, Hellenic Ministries. Along with other groups, they have been present on Lesvos feeding and providing shelter for these homeless refugee families. It came as quite a surprise when Lornie, originally part of our Paros group, announced that she felt led to go and help them. Having left Paros years before, she had remained in England after her mother's death. Now at last her fluent Greek and her passion for sharing the love of Jesus could be put to good use with the refugees. For many, it would have been enough to serve as a volunteer for a few weeks or months, but Lornie felt compelled to pack up and leave her home for as many years as the Lord would use her. Her stories of events in the camps were heart rending; none more so than the night all the tents were burned down. The next day, there was Lornie with her rake, preparing the scorched earth with fresh gravel and spraying to make it fit to re-erect tents. After months toiling in the refugee camps of Lesvos, she left to begin her pre-arranged voluntary work in Athens with Operation Mobilisation, another world wide organisation. To offer her services to these organisations, she has found those willing to support her day to day needs for food and, now, rent as she lives in the centre of Athens at the heart of the crisis. Her many hours of service offer her no financial reward, so even the lowly paid pensioner or supermarket worker has a greater salary than she. Her reward will be before the throne of God when He says, "Well done, my good and faithful servant".

To most Greek Orthodox people, these organisations are unknown and treated with suspicion because they are outside the Orthodox Church. To the hungry refugee, they are the difference between life and death, starving or being fed. We live in hope that, one day, all the Christians of God's world will rise above their denominational divisions and work together as one. It is evident that the crisis of refugees and homeless Greeks shows little sign of subsiding and that God needs our hands to show His love to these struggling souls.

Christians from around the world have flown into Athens to set up an International House of Prayer. They plan to pray 24/7 for the Greek nation, the refugees and the homeless. God is sending workers into the harvest to answer the heart cry of the needy in Greece.

ABOUT THE AUTHOR

Barbara graduated from Manchester University in 1973, with a degree in computing and management science. For many years she pursued a successful career in computing with international banks and multinational companies.

While on holiday in the Greek Islands she had a dramatic, life changing experience. This resulted in her leaving her work in England at the age of thirty-seven, to embark on a journey of faith living on the Greek island of Paros.

Her life in Greece has provided her with many hilarious Greek experiences, knowledge of the local Greek culture and a wealth of miracles of provision, supernatural guidance and healings.

Initially living alone, she later met and married her Belgian husband. Together they built their home close to the beach which became a lighthouse to people of many nationalities. Many lives have been touched through their weekly meetings.

Barbara has been living on the island of Paros for more than twenty five years.

She lives an extraordinary life in a simple island setting.

46487222R00126

Made in the USA
Middletown, DE
29 May 2019